Miracle·Gro®

Water Gardens

Simple steps to building garden pools & fountains

Meredith® Books
Des Moines, Iowa

Miracle-Gro Basics - Water Gardens
Writer: Megan McConnell Hughes
Editor: Marilyn Rogers
Contributing Designer: Studio G Design
Copy Chief: Terri Fredrickson
Publishing Operations Manager: Karen Schirm
Senior Editor, Asset and Information Manager: Phillip Morgan
Edit and Design Production Coordinator: Mary Lee Gavin
Editorial Assistant: Kathleen Stevens
Book Production Managers: Pam Kvitne, Marjorie J. Schenkelberg, Rick von Holdt, Mark Weaver
Contributing Copy Editor: Sarah Oliver Watson
Contributing Proofreaders: Stephanie Petersen
Contributing Photographers: Aquascape Designs, Inc.: Cover, 91; Becket Corporation: 70, 71;
    Flora Graphics: 38T, 39T; GardenWorld Images: 46BR; Susan M. Glascock: 38B; Lynne
    Harrison: 55corner, 55B; Rosemary Kautzky: 1, 54, 74, 75, 76, 77; David Liebman/Quality
    Nature Photography: 62B; Hanson Man: 62BC; J. Paul Moore: 46CR; Greg Speichert: 39B;
    Albert Squillace/Positive Images: 46TR
Contributing Photo Researcher: Susan Ferguson
Contributing Photo Stylist: Diane Witosky
Indexer: Richard T. Evans, Infodex Indexing Services Inc.
Special thanks to: Earl May Nursery and Garden Center, Mary Irene Swartz

Meredith® Books
Executive Director, Editorial: Gregory H. Kayko
Executive Director, Design: Matt Strelecki
Managing Editor: Amy Tincher-Durik
Executive Editor/Group Manager: Benjamin W. Allen
Senior Associate Design Director: Ken Carlson
Marketing Product Manager: Isaac Petersen

Publisher and Editor in Chief: James D. Blume
Editorial Director: Linda Raglan Cunningham
Executive Director, New Business Development: Todd M. Davis
Executive Director, Sales: Ken Zagor
Director, Operations: George A. Susral
Director, Production: Douglas M. Johnston
Director, Marketing: Amy Nichols
Business Director: Jim Leonard

Vice President and General Manager: Douglas J. Guendel

Meredith Publishing Group
President: Jack Griffin
Executive Vice President: Bob Mate

Meredith Corporation
Chairman and Chief Executive Officer: William T. Kerr
President and Chief Operating Officer: Stephen M. Lacy

In Memoriam: E.T. Meredith III (1933-2003)

If you would like more information on other Miracle-Gro products, call 800/225-2883 or visit us
at: www.miraclegro.com

All of us at Meredith® Books are dedicated to providing you with information and ideas to
enhance your home and garden. We welcome your comments and suggestions. Write to us at:
Meredith Books, Garden Editorial Department, 1716 Locust St., Des Moines, IA 50309-3023.

Note to the Readers: Due to differing conditions, tools, and individual skills, Meredith
Corporation assumes no responsibility for any damages, injuries suffered, or losses incurred as a
result of following the information published in this book. Before beginning any project, review
the instructions carefully, and if any doubts or questions remain, consult local experts or
authorities.

Dive In!

Recent innovations make it easier than ever to plunge into the world of water gardening. Trickling fountains and tabletop water gardens are perfect oases for apartment dwellers. A balcony or patio is an ideal spot for a small container water garden. And the average residential lot offers dozens of possibilities for a range of creative water features teeming with flora and fauna.

This book is filled with all the basics you need to successfully build your own simple water garden. You'll find step-by-step information for eight projects, as well as a gallery of excellent water garden plants.

< 3 >

HOW TO USE THIS BOOK

This handy, go-anywhere waterproof book takes you through the process of designing and building your own water feature. Whether you choose to create one of the water projects beginning on page 63 or build your own unique feature, this book is stocked with timely tips and essential advice for an easy-care garden pool.

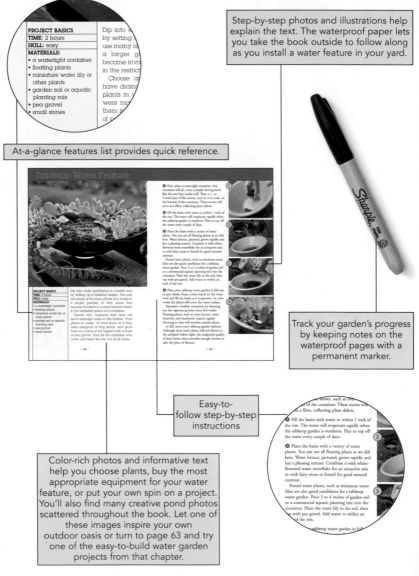

Step-by-step photos and illustrations help explain the text. The waterproof paper lets you take the book outside to follow along as you install a water feature in your yard.

At-a-glance features list provides quick reference.

Track your garden's progress by keeping notes on the waterproof pages with a permanent marker.

Easy-to-follow step-by-step instructions

Color-rich photos and informative text help you choose plants, buy the most appropriate equipment for your water feature, or put your own spin on a project. You'll also find many creative pond photos scattered throughout the book. Let one of these images inspire your own outdoor oasis or turn to page 63 and try one of the easy-to-build water garden projects from that chapter.

< 4 >

Any watertight container—from a ceramic pot to an old pair of rubber boots—can host a water garden. Small vessels make excellent portable water gardens you can tote to areas needing a splash of interest. Larger containers, such as whiskey barrels, galvanized tubs, and hefty urns can visually anchor the corner of a patio or a garden bed.

Plant container water gardens with a variety of water garden plants. Floating plants are particularly well-suited for tabletop water gardens, while potted plants do best in large containers. Large containers can also host goldfish. For a healthy water garden ecosystem the container should hold at least 5 gallons of water per inch of fish.

< 6 >

Container Garden Basics

OPTIMAL SITE: Container water gardens are at home on porches, on patios, and in the landscape. These movable water wonders are ideal easy-care gardens for small spaces.

INSTALLATION NOTES: A simple container water garden consists of a watertight vessel, water, plants, and fish, if desired. Create a gurgling container water garden by adding a pump and fountain head. The pump requires electricity, so plan on placing a container garden that has moving water near a power source.

CARE REQUIREMENTS: Container gardens require a few minutes of maintenance weekly during the growing season. Where winter temperatures regularly dip below freezing, container water gardens need to be brought indoors. You can keep a small container water garden going in your home over the winter or store it. If the garden contains plants, place it near a sunny window. Disassemble a large water garden and store the components in a garage or shed until spring. Perennial plants can be overwintered. See pages 88 and 89 for more information.

COST: Container water gardens generally require only a small monetary investment. You can create a stellar tabletop garden for less than $20. Ornate container gardens, those with fountains and plants, can exceed $100.

Small Ponds

Ponds and pools are what most people think of when they hear the term "water garden." Although a water garden can be as simple as a birdbath, moving up to a small pond will allow you to try your hand at growing a variety of water-loving plants and aquatic animals right outside your door.

A basic size guideline for a small pond is at least 50 square feet of surface area with a minimum depth of 18 inches. (Ponds should be at least 2 feet deep in cold climates.) A pond this size has moderate temperature swings, provides plenty of room for plants and a few fish, and is less prone to algae growth. Fifty square feet translates to a 10×5-foot rectangular pool or an 8-foot-diameter circular one. If the water feature is strictly decorative, with no fish and few plants, dimensions are less critical.

A small garden pool is ideal for a small lot but will be lost in an expansive landscape unless sited carefully. In large landscapes, locate a small water feature near a porch or patio so you can enjoy it up close. Be sure electricity is accessible for pumps and fountains.

Small Pond Basics

OPTIMAL SITE: Small ponds are easiest to install on a level site. Although low spots might seem ideal for water features, they collect runoff from lawns and are prone to flooding.

INSTALLATION NOTES: Small water gardens are available in kits, complete with a flexible or preformed liner, pump, filter, and fountain. You can also purchase separate components for a unique look.

Two people can install a small pond in a weekend. If the soil surrounding the pond is clay, plan to work three days or more due to the challenging digging.

CARE REQUIREMENTS: A small pond requires one to two hours of care a week during the growing season. In areas where temperatures can drop as low as –20°F, it is best to build a 2-foot-deep pond to ease winter care. At this depth, water will not usually freeze solid, so plants and fish can overwinter in the pond.

COST: On average, a do-it-yourselfer can install a small pond garden for $800 to $1,500.

Large Ponds

As the size of a pond increases, the number of plants and fish it can support increases as well. An expansive pond allows you to host a multitude of water lilies, lotuses, iris, and other water plants, or to build a fish lovers' fantasy stocked with a rainbow of swimmers. For plant or fish collectors, a large pond is a must.

Although a large pond has a greater surface area than a small 10×5-foot pond, it typically requires no more care. A large pond is likely to support a thriving ecosystem, which keeps plant and animal populations in check. Balance is key. When plant and aquatic animal populations are in balance, they essentially will maintain the pond for you by devouring debris, oxygenating the water, and limiting growth of pests.

Before diving into a large pond project, hone your pond skills with a container water garden or small pond. Use these small water gardens to learn as much as you can about how to create a balanced ecosystem in your climate before building a large pond. Once it is established, your large pond will require just one to two hours of care a week.

Large Pond Basics

OPTIMAL SITE: A level site in full sun is best. Position the pond where you will enjoy it most—for example, near a deck or a porch. However, the larger size means the pond doesn't have to be right next to its viewing area. Keep the size of the pond in scale with its surroundings. Make the pond a destination in the landscape by creating waterside seating or a dining area.

INSTALLATION NOTES: Consider working with a skilled landscape architect or water garden specialist to design a pleasing pond and head off any challenges your site might present. Digging a large pond can be time-consuming, strenuous work. Enlist the help of three or four strong friends and have a pond-digging party. Or hire an excavator to carve out the water hole. You can then fine-tune the shape, lay the liner, and finish the pond. Don't forget that your pond will require electricity to run pumps and filters. Hire a skilled electrician to run electricity to the pond if needed.

CARE REQUIREMENTS: A large pond with a balance of plants and aquatic animals requires two or more hours of care a week.

COST: Plan to invest $2,000 or more to install a simple 10×20-foot water garden with a small fountain and several plants.

Waterfalls and Streams

The best waterfalls and streams appear to spring naturally from the landscape. For design inspiration, check out rocky, gurgling streams flowing down hills or mountains and compare them with calmer, meandering creeks. Notice how rocks and other obstacles affect their current speed and direction. Position rocks and plants in the water in the same way they occur in nature to give the watercourse a natural appearance.

Streams and waterfalls provide solutions for difficult-to-landscape areas, such as steep slopes, rocky terrain, and areas of deep shade. A stream connecting two pools can turn your yard into a welcome oasis for plants and animals and a restful retreat for you.

Streams and waterfalls require advanced installation skills, but with careful planning you can enjoy the music of moving water in your own yard. Get started with the help of a friend who is familiar with building streams and waterfalls. Or consult a water garden professional for advice.

Waterfall and Stream Basics

OPTIMAL SITE: Waterfalls and streams look natural when built on a slope. A gentle slope with a 1- to 2-inch vertical drop for every 10 feet of length provides adequate flow for a stream.

INSTALLATION NOTES: As with large ponds, you might want to consider working with a skilled landscape architect or water garden specialist. Once you know the shape of your water feature, the steps involved include digging header ponds and catch basins (where the water will begin to flow and stop flowing in a stream). Next you'll need to excavate the stream and use stones to build a waterfall if one is part of the design. For the water from the foot of the stream or waterfall to return to the head, you'll need to dig a 6-inch-deep trench alongside the stream for the piping. And finally you'll need to add a trench for electricity. Hire an electrician to run a line to the feature.

CARE REQUIREMENTS: A waterfall or stream requires two or more hours of maintenance a week.

COST: Plan to invest $1,500 or more in a stream or waterfall.

< 13 >

Fountains

If the sound of moving water is music to your ears, a fountain will be a wonderful addition to your landscape. Install a pump to add a fountain to your existing water garden, or consider a free-standing fountain for your deck, patio, or garden. Fountains are available in a multitude of styles and sizes. Depending on the size of the water feature and your climate, you may need to disassemble and store the fountain during winter.

Fountain Basics

OPTIMAL SITE: Place a fountain near a window or an outdoor seating area for maximum enjoyment.

INSTALLATION NOTES: A freestanding fountain can be installed in a day or less. You'll need electricity, of course, to power the fountain.

CARE REQUIREMENTS: Fountains require only a few minutes of maintenance weekly.

COST: Purchase and install a fountain for as little as $50.

< 14 >

< 15 >

Select a Site

Build your water garden in a prime location to minimize maintenance and maximize your enjoyment. Begin choosing a location by considering how you will use the water feature. Do you want to look out your living room window to see a waterfall? Or perhaps you would like to add a tranquil pond to your outdoor dining area. Placing a water garden in a location where you will enjoy it daily will help you remember to care for it.

Before you decide on the location, keep in mind slope, soil, sun, shade, wind, and location of utility lines. Finding the perfect spot requires balancing all of these elements. Here's what to look for in a good site for a water feature:

SLOPE Consider the slope and grade of your yard and work with it. The lowest spot may look like the best place for a pond, but it's actually the worst. Rainwater flows into a low-lying pond, where it will muddy the water, wash away fish, and knock over plants. Place the pond just above the lowest spot to avoid these problems.

A slope, however, might be the perfect spot for a waterfall or stream. When building on a slope, make sure you have a clear, safe, and easy path on which to carry materials to the pond site.

SOIL Installation can be easy or difficult, depending on the kind of soil you have. If the soil is especially hard and rocky, save yourself the digging and install an aboveground feature.

Sandy soil poses problems as well. The soil may cave in along the sides of the pond as you try to install a flexible-liner in-ground pond. In such cases, a preformed liner may be the answer.

Clay soil, although sometimes difficult to excavate, can be ideal for in-ground installations. Because clay soil holds its shape, flexible liners will conform to whatever configuration you dig.

SUN, SHADE, AND WIND Take an inventory of the sun and shade patterns in your yard so you can make sure your water garden plants get the sunlight (or the shade) they require. Most water plants require at least six hours of direct sunlight each day.

Wind can affect plant life too. Strong winds speed evaporation from the pond and can break the stems of some tender plants and harm plants that thrive in tranquil water. If you must locate the pond in a windy spot, erect a windscreen or plant shrubs as a natural wall.

< 16 >

UTILITIES Avoid locating your water feature over electrical, water, sewer, or gas lines. Also consider how you will get water and electricity to the garden. The closer it is to an existing electrical outlet or wiring, the less expensive it will be to run a line to it, if necessary. Running a water line to the feature is only necessary if you can't reach the feature with a garden hose to top off the water level.

< 17 >

1 Although garden ponds are as unique as their owners, they all have a couple of things in common. All ponds have an underlayment and liner. The liner acts as a basin to prevent pond water from seeping out and groundwater from seeping in. The underlayment provides protection for the liner, cushioning it from rocks and other sharp objects. All ponds are surrounded by edging material, **2** which secures the edge of the liner.

Moving beyond liners and underlayment, ponds include many different components and features. Here is a sampling of popular pond features:

1 SHELVES Many marginal plants grow best in shallow water, and a shelf cut into the sides of the pond puts them at the right depth. The shelves might circle the pond or be formed on only a portion of the outline. Typically they start 8 to 10 inches below the water surface and can be up to 12 inches deep.

PUMPS Ponds with moving water must include a pump. Powered by electricity, pumps allow streams to flow, fountains to spray, ponds to drain, and water to circulate.

2 FOUNTAIN HEADS Also called spray heads, fountain heads work in combination with a pump to bubble or spray water in a pond. They aerate the water, which keeps fish alive, help cut down on algae growth, and contribute to a healthy ecosystem. Consider the needs of plants when choosing a pump. Many, such as water lilies, don't like water on their leaves and prefer an undisturbed surface.

< 18 >

When choosing a fountain head, first consider the height and width of its spray pattern, although you can often adjust both with a valve on the pump. Second, choose the style that fits the appearance of your water feature. A bubbler, for example, looks natural in a small informal water garden tucked into a perennial border.

3 SKIMMERS AND FILTERS These small pond components are not required for a healthy ecosystem but often provide aesthetic enjoyment and simplify maintenance chores. Skimmers help maintain water quality by removing floating leaves and other debris before they decay and sink to the bottom of the pond. Filters strain debris out of the water to keep it liquid clear.

Anatomy of a Garden Pond

1 EDGING SHELF Stones attractively mask the edge of this pond. The edging shelf smooths the transition from the pond to the surrounding landscape by partially submerging the stones.

2 UNDERLAYMENT A valuable cushion under the liner, the underlayment (shown here in orange) protects the liner from punctures.

3 LINER Made of rigid or flexible plastic, the liner creates the pond reservoir. (shown here as thin black line between underlayment and water)

4 EDGING This pond has a combination of pebble and rock edging.

5 DEEP ZONE A deep zone is at least 36 inches deep and is used to overwinter fish and hardy plants in cold climates.

6 MARGINAL SHELF Plants that prefer to grow in shallow water, thrive on a 12-inch-deep marginal shelf.

Flexible Liners

With the help of a flexible liner you can build pools, streams, and waterfalls in just about any shape, length, and style imaginable. Developed in the 1960s to replace concrete and other pond building materials, flexible liners are one of the most important innovations in garden pond technology. Flexible liner is so easy to use that one person can install a small water garden with little effort. The most time-consuming task is folding the excess.

Flexible liners come in a variety of materials—polyethylene, polyvinyl chloride (PVC), and ethylene propylene diene monomer (EPDM). They also vary greatly in thickness, cost, and quality. Heavier liners are generally more expensive, more durable, and more puncture- and tear-resistant than lighter-weight liners. However, new liner developments combine durability with less weight. As a rule, the more you spend, the more the liner will resist the sun's ultraviolet rays, which break down liners. Pond liners average 25 to 75 cents per square foot.

Most liners come in black, a color well suited to garden pools. Black is natural-looking and blends with the algae that will cover it after a few months. (The algae cover helps liners resist UV damage.) Black also gives a pool the illusion of greater depth.

Stock sizes for liners range from 5-foot squares up to sections 50 by 100 feet or larger. You can create streams and other large features by joining pieces with tape or sealer made specifically for this purpose.

When buying a liner, make sure it is safe for use with plants and fish. Liners for other uses (swimming pools or roofs, for example) are toxic.

Underlayment

All liners require the installation of an underlayment, a cushion of material between the liner and the soil that prevents punctures and tears. Sand is a good choice for the pool bottom and other horizontal surfaces but can't be laid vertically. Old carpet and underlayment made specifically for ponds are ideal. Some new liners are manufactured with an underlayment already attached. They are extremely puncture-resistant and can be used, for example, over coarse gravel or sharp rock.

If a liner does tear or puncture, it's no cause for alarm. You can repair it with a patch and solvent cement. However, you'll have to drain the pool first, clean the area, and let it dry so the patch will stick to the liner. Prevent rips and tears when working on the pond by wearing soft-sole shoes or just socks.

< 20 >

How to Calculate the Liner Size
Flexible liners are often purchased by the square foot. Determine the size of your water feature before you purchase a liner for it.

HERE'S HOW:
• Imagine your pond as a rectangle, even though it may be round or irregular. Make sure the rectangle includes the farthest points of the pond. Then consider the depth of the pond.

• The liner size equals the length plus two times the depth, plus 2 feet, multiplied by the width plus two times the depth, plus 2 feet. This allows for a 1-foot overlap around the perimeter.

• For example, a pond that measures 15 feet by 10 feet and is 1½ feet deep needs a liner that is 20 feet long (15+1½+1½+2 = 20) by 15 feet wide (10+1½+1½+2 = 15). 20 feet times 15 feet = a 300-square-foot liner.

Preformed Liners

Easy to install and well suited to small garden ponds, preformed liners (also called rigid liners) are available in many ready-made sizes and styles. Preformed liners are much more durable than flexible liners and are easier to repair if damaged.

Preformed liners are ideal in areas where stony soil or tree roots prevent or hinder excavation. You can place them entirely above ground or install them at any depth. But don't expect aboveground liners to support themselves. They need a structure built around them to push against the weight of the water.

Most preformed liners are constructed of fiberglass or rigid plastic. Fiberglass is more expensive but lasts longer than rigid plastic. A small 6×3-foot fiberglass liner starts at around $300, compared with $100 for a rigid-plastic liner. Large fiberglass liners can cost $900 or more. Properly installed, they can last as long as 50 years. Rigid-plastic liners, on the other hand, last about 20 years.

Rigid-plastic liners are by far the most common and can be found at garden centers and home improvement stores. In addition to being readily accessible, rigid liners are available in a vast number of sizes and shapes making it easy to find the perfect style for your landscape.

Preformed liners are available in many shapes, formal and informal. Standard preformed liners come in a variety of depths; some include shallow ledges for marginal plants and deep zones in which fish overwinter. Although you can buy preformed units in different colors, black is usually best for the same reasons as it is for a flexible liner: It's neutral and creates the illusion that the pool is deeper than it actually is. If the wide variety of ready-made shapes doesn't suit you, shop around for a manufacturer to custom-make one for you.

Install Carefully

Installing a preformed liner takes more care than a flexible liner. Using excavated soil, backfill around the liner. Make sure the unit is absolutely level so the water in the pool will be level. Also, be sure to backfill any nooks and crevices so the plastic doesn't collapse under the weight of the water. Take care when using heavy edging, such as stone. Some preformed liner edges are convex with a little upward curve to them. Because the curve can't be supported underneath, the weight of the stone will crush them. Other edges are designed to bear weight (check with the supplier), but they must be fully supported with backfill.

< 22 >

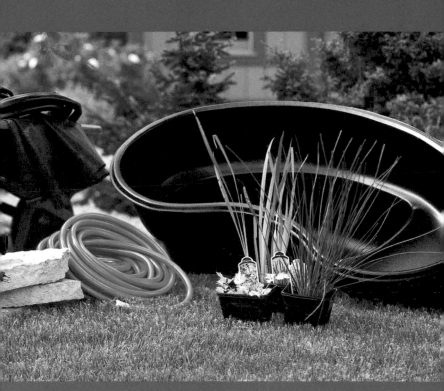

Flexible vs. Preformed Liners

	Flexible	Preformed
Landscape use	Excellent for free-form water features, lining an existing water garden to make it watertight, and other in-ground projects.	Can be installed in ground or above ground; ideal for hard-to-excavate areas; best for small features.
Sizes and shapes available	Use to create a water garden of any size or shape.	A limited variety of shapes and sizes available.
Typical life span	PVC liners: 10 years or more. EPDM liners: 20 years or more.	Rigid-plastic liners: at least 20 years. Fiberglass liners: 50 years or more.
Approximate cost of a 6×3-foot pond liner	$70 to $125 depending on the type.	Rigid-plastic liner: $100. Fiberglass liner: $300.

Pumps

Moving water through a water feature once required complicated plumbing. Today, all you need is a pump. Its installation takes just minutes to assemble and set in your pond. Use a pump to power a filter, circulate water, and send a fountain head into motion.

Selecting a pump

Water garden pumps are available in submersible and external models. In both, the mechanism is simply a set of whirling blades that pressurize the water and force it into motion. Submersible pumps are easier to use than external pumps and they are less expensive. They sit directly in the water, unlike external pumps, which you have to locate outside the pond. Submersible pumps can be used for all but the largest water features.

The most important aspect when choosing a pump is its size. The critical measure of pump power is the number of gallons of water it will pump per hour to a specific height; this is called the head.

To determine the size of pump you'll need, first calculate the volume of water in the pond. An easy way to do this after you've dug and lined the pond is to jot down the reading on your water meter. Then fill the garden pond and note the new reading. Most meters measure the amount of water used in cubic feet. Convert it to gallons by multiplying by 7.48. If this method is not an option for you, consult a local water garden specialist for help in determining the volume of your pond.

As a rule, it's best to choose a pump that can move half the total volume of water in an hour. For example, if your pond will hold 500 gallons of water, buy a pump that delivers at least 250 gallons of water an hour. Fountain heads often have pump size recommendations.

Other considerations

Buy the best quality pump you can afford. Pumps with plastic housings are the least expensive and least durable. Brass, bronze, and stainless steel housings last longer. Aluminum housings will eventually corrode.

Pumps have varying lengths of cord; check to make sure the cord is long enough to reach from the outlet to the center of the pond. The longer the cord, the better, especially because some codes specify that the electrical outlet for a water feature be at least 6 feet away.

Finally, be sure to buy a pump that is designed for use in a water garden. Unlike other types of pumps, those for water gardens sustain continuous, round-the-clock use.

< 24 >

A Note About Filters

Filters keep water clear and prevent your pumps from clogging with water-garden debris—fish waste, decayed organic matter, floating algae, leftover fish food, and many other unwanted tiny particles.

Not every garden pond that's home to fish and plants will need a filter, because a well-balanced ecosystem usually "cleans" itself sufficiently. If you can tolerate water that's less than clear, so can the plants and fish. But if the garden pond you are planning will be home to fish and not plants, you'll have to install a filter to clean up after them.

The type and number of filters needed depend both on your tolerance for murky water and the kind of water feature you have. After planning and designing your water feature, consult with your water garden supplier to learn which filter is best.

Edging

Selecting and installing the right edging for your water garden is critical. Edging hides the liner; at the same time it defines the style of your garden pond and sets its mood. As you choose edging, consider the following:

❶ Turf

Turf makes a striking edging for formal ponds set in a flat stretch of lawn. It costs little, is easy to install, and is a good choice for edging an in-ground preformed liner with a lip that is not designed to support much weight. If you are seeding a new lawn, install sod around the pond to prevent soil from washing into the water.

Use turf as an edging only when you can keep the surrounding lawn in excellent condition; a brown or spotted lawn will be a splotchy frame for your water garden. Be aware, too, that having a water feature within the lawn can complicate lawn care. Use fertilizer and pesticides in moderation around a pond to avoid algae growth in the water. If the pond is stocked with fish, use only fish-safe materials.

❷ Flagstone

Flagstone combines well with boulders, gravel, sand, or rock in naturalistic settings. It's easy to install as edging and ideal for a variety of water features—including ones on slopes—because you can stack it. It is also excellent for securing flexible liners in place and it can be mortared for stability and permanence.

< 26 >

Limestone is the most popular flagstone. Its appearance improves as it weathers and as moss and algae grow on it.

To use flagstone, dig a shallow shelf around the pool. Experiment with placing the pieces so they fit together neatly. Local stone is the least expensive ($1 or less per square foot) and often the most natural looking.

❸ Brick and concrete pavers

Using brick and concrete pavers is a great way to tie in with the patios, walks, or other hardscapes in your yard. Depending on the method you use, installing brick and concrete pavers can be easy or a challenge. It's fairly easy to dry lay them in sand, for example, but more difficult to set them in concrete.

❹ Cut stone

Cut stone is more expensive and more formal in appearance than flagstone, and it looks most appropriate around square or rectangular pools. It is excellent in most formal gardens, and it blends well with gravel, wood, brick, and other materials, both formal and informal.

❺ Boulders

Ideal for naturalistic ponds, small boulders are relatively easy to work with. You'll need help to move any large boulders you want to install, and unless you find a free supply, purchase price and delivery costs will be high.

❻ Patios and decking

Water features built into a patio or deck put the water at a level where it's easy to enjoy. You won't have to buy separate edging material for the pond, so a deck or patio addition will be relatively inexpensive. Make sure the wood has not been treated with preservatives that can leach into the water and harm plants or fish.

< 27 >

Digging a Pond

The most daunting part of creating a large garden pond is the digging. But with some planning, digging can be downright fun.

Plan the project

1 When planning your garden pond, take into consideration how much digging you have the ability to do and adjust either the size of the water garden or the amount you do by yourself.

Consider hiring a neighborhood teen or enlist friends and relatives to help out. For a large project, you may want to hire a backhoe operator. As a rule, water gardens with a surface area of less than 250 square feet are most economically built by hand; large projects are

2 best done with a backhoe.

Allow plenty of time for digging, considering pool size and soil type. A small 18-inch-deep 3×5-foot pool in sandy soil may take only an hour, while a similar size pond in clay soil can take four or more hours to dig.

Make sure your tools are in excellent condition and well-suited to the task. You'll need a sharp spade, a wheelbarrow for hauling dirt, and possibly a truck for hauling away soil.

< 28 >

Digging a pond step-by-step

1 MARK THE OUTLINE of the pond with a garden hose or rope. Live with the outline for a week or so to discover how well the new feature fits into the landscape and how it will affect traffic patterns.

2 REMOVE TURF. Use it to fill bare spots in the lawn or set it aside in a pile of its own to compost. If you have taken up a large quantity of turf, consider using it as the base of a berm or a raised bed.

3 AS YOU DIG keep the pond edge level; otherwise the liner will show when the pond is filled. Check by resting a carpenter's level on a straight board laid across the pond. Work all around the pond, checking every shelf and side of the pool so that there are no surprises.

4 CREATE A SPOT to overwinter plants and fish. In cold areas, you'll need a zone in the pool that won't freeze. It should be up to 3 feet deep and as wide as it is deep. Be sure this deep zone isn't in the same spot you want to place a pump or fountain.

5 DIG AN 8- TO 12-INCH SHELF for marginal plants around the edge of the pond. Position the shelf so that the plants will frame your view of the water garden. Then dig a ledge for the edging as deep as the edging material and slightly less wide.

6 TOSS THE EXCAVATED SOIL into a wheelbarrow or onto a tarp to protect your lawn. If it's in good condition, use it to fill in other spots in the landscape, build a slope for a waterfall, or haul it to a construction site that needs fill dirt.

< 29 >

Flexible liners have become popular largely because they are easy to install. However, you must install it properly to prevent the liner from showing (which speeds UV deterioration) and leaks from developing.

Begin by removing any rough edges in the freshly dug pond. Discard roots, rocks, debris, and buried shards of glass—anything that might puncture the liner. Spread the liner in the sun for an hour or two to let it soften, which makes it much easier to handle. If you need to seam two pieces, do it now, using solvent cement or an adhesive designed for this purpose. Enlist a few friends to help you move the liner.

Installing a flexible liner step-by-step

1 ❶ CUSHION THE HOLE WITH UNDERLAYMENT. Use moist sand, old carpet, or commercial underlayment made for water gardens to cover the bottom and sides of the pool. Laying underlayment can be frustrating; cut triangles at corners and curves to help fit contours. Underlayment should be ½ to 2 inches thick, depending on the material.

< 30 >

2 POSITION THE LINER. After the liner has softened in the sun, drape it loosely in the hole, arranging and pleating as needed. (This may be a job for two or more people.) Try flapping it like a sheet (up and down) to force air under the liner and help it float into place. Anchor the sides with bricks or stones, taking care not to stretch the liner.

3 ADJUST THE LINER. Add a few inches of water to the pool to settle the liner. Pleat and tuck the liner as necessary to make it fit the contours and corners of the water feature. Leave a little wrinkle of extra liner in the bottom of the pond. This allows the liner to spread a little when the soil settles.

4 PREPARE FOR EDGING. Fill the pond with a few more inches of water. Adjust the liner, pleating here and there as necessary, and then fill to just below the edging shelf. Use heavy scissors or a utility knife to trim the liner, leaving as much excess liner as possible over the outside edge of the pool.

5 INSTALL EDGING. Use your choice of flagstone, brick, cut stone, or other material. Here's a good way to prevent the liner from showing: Dig the edging shelf deep enough for a double layer of flagstones, cut stones, bricks, or other edging, then wrap the liner over the first layer and top with the second. Water can now be filled to the middle of the first layer of edging. With one layer of edging, the water can be filled to only a little below the bottom of the edging material.

Finish by trimming excess liner. You can pat a little soil in behind the edging to conceal any visible liner.

< 31 >

Installing a Preformed Liner

Although rigid liner is a little more difficult to install than flexible liner, it's relatively simple. The key is ensuring the liner is level at all times, using a carpenter's level and a straight board.

Installation step-by-step

1 **POSITION THE LINER** where you plan to locate the pond, using bricks if necessary to keep the liner level. Pound stakes in place around the lip of the liner and use them as a guide to mark the liner's exact outline. If the pool is small, you can make a template by turning the liner over on a sheet of cardboard and tracing around the outside of the lip.

< 32 >

2 DIG OUT THE SHAPE of the liner, making it 2 inches wider and 2 to 3 inches deeper than the actual liner. Conform your digging to the shape of the shelves and deep zones, measuring depth, width, and level frequently. Monitor your work by lowering the liner into place every so often and making adjustments as needed.

3 ONCE THE HOLE IS DUG, make sure there aren't any sharp objects or stones left on the bottom. Spread a layer of moist sand, fine soil, or a combination of the two over the bottom of the hole to cushion the liner. Use a short board as a screed to level the bottom. Firmly tamp down the sand or soil and recheck the level. Be sure to fill all voids and pockets, especially around and under the marginal shelves.

4 LOWER THE LINER INTO PLACE, again checking the level. You may need to remove the liner several times to adjust the depth of the hole until the liner is level all the way around.

5 ONCE THE POND IS PERFECTLY LEVEL, add 4 inches of water to the liner and begin backfilling around the pond with a mixture of sand and soil, checking the level as you go. Tamp the soil with a shovel handle or 2×4 as you work. Backfill again and add 4 more inches of water, keeping the water level no higher than the backfill. Repeat until the pond is filled.

Make preparations for edging. If the liner has a flat lip, work a foundation of crushed stone topped with damp sand under the lip and around the liner edges. Then position the stone or other edging on top. If the lip can't support heavy edging, pour a 3- to 4-inch-deep concrete footing around the liner. Spread mortar on the footing, then set the edging in it so that it overhangs the lip of the pond.

< 33 >

A Word About Water

All local water supplies contain some form of chemical disinfectant, usually chlorine or chloramines. (Chloramines also occur in water naturally.) These disinfectants may be present alone or in combination.

These chemicals do not harm plants, but they do harm wildlife (fish, snails, and frogs, for example). It's best to remove disinfectants in a new pond, even if you don't plan to stock fish.

Before you introduce fish or plants, check with your water supplier to see which disinfectants are present in your water. Then take these steps to remove them.

USE A DECHLORINATOR to remove chlorine, or let the water in your pond stand for five to seven days to allow the chlorine to dissipate before stocking the pond.

TREAT THE WATER WITH A CHLORAMINE REMOVER, which also takes out chlorine. You can purchase a chloramine remover at a water garden supply house. The action of dechlorinators and chloramine removers is almost immediate—you can introduce fish to the pool shortly after using either one.

Use a dechlorinator and a chloramine remover when stocking a new pond and when refilling the pond after cleaning.

WHEN TOPPING OFF THE POND (to replace evaporation, for example), you don't need to treat tap water. Simply follow these steps:

• Place the hose in the bottom of the pond.

• Add water slowly, in a trickle, to avoid shocking the fish and to prevent them from being attracted to the activity of the water bubbles.

• Add no more than 10 to 20 percent of the water at a time.

< 34 >

Aquatic Life

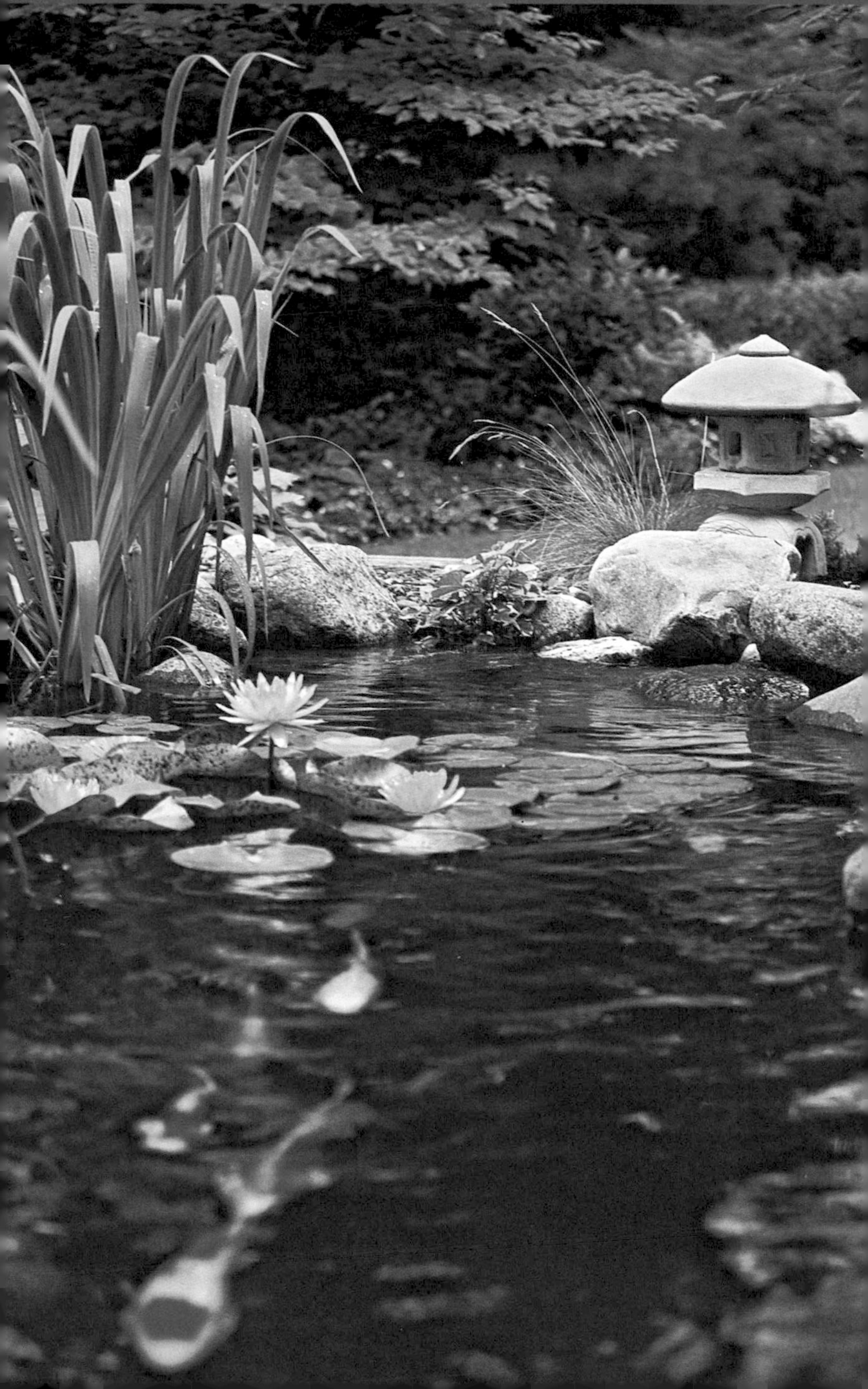

Choosing Plants

Water plants come in all shapes and sizes. Some grow completely underwater; others only want their toes wet. Depending on how and where they grow in the pond, water garden plants fall into five categories.

❶ Submerged plants

Aquatics whose roots are anchored in soil and whose foliage grows entirely underwater are called submerged water plants. Many submerged water plants have colorful foliage that glistens underwater, and several have flowers that float on or rise just above the water surface during summer. Most submerged plants thrive in water up to 10 feet deep.

❷ Floating plants

Floating plants sit on the water surface with no need of pot or soil. Their roots dangle in the water, drawing nutrients from it. They have an important role in the water garden, absorbing the nitrogen and phosphates that result from the breakdown of fish waste and plant debris that would otherwise promote algae growth.

Floaters are extremely easy to grow and are the least expensive water plants, so treat them as annuals and buy them fresh each year.

❸ Water lilies

Water lilies grow with their roots in soil below the water surface, and their round leaves, which look like green platters, floating on the water. Some cultivars have floating flowers; others hold their blooms on stems several inches above the water.

Water lilies prefer water that is nearly or completely still. Most grow in 3- to 4-foot depths, but they can do well in ponds with only 6 to 18 inches of water over their roots.

Water lilies fall into two broad groups. Hardy water lilies survive winters in cold climates. Tropical water lilies cannot withstand a winter freeze and need special care during cold months.

④ Lotuses

Lotuses are similar to water lilies, growing in wet soil in water up to 3 feet deep. But unlike water lilies, they hold some of their leaves and all of their flowers well above the water. Lotus leaves are round and either float or stand out of the water like inverted parasols. Lotus cultivars grow from 6 inches to 6 feet tall.

⑤ Marginals

Marginals grow at the edge, or margin, of the pond, in shallow water or in saturated to just-moist soil. Their roots are in soil while most of their foliage rises out of the water. Many marginals can adapt to the perennial garden, as long as the soil is fairly moist, making them ideal transitional plants that link the pond with other gardens.

Beware of Unruly Plants

Before you buy a plant, find out how well behaved it is. Water garden plants, especially floaters, have a tendency to be invasive in ideal climates. In fact, some are banned from states where they can escape the garden and flourish and clog natural waterways. Invasive plants also can be a maintenance headache in a water garden. They'll battle you for control, and you'll spend hours pulling them out of the pond.

HORNWORT

FANWORT

SUBMERGED PLANT FEATURES

PLANTING DEPTH: the bottom of the pond; specific depth varies

LIGHT: sun to part shade

PLANT TYPE: grow as annual

>improve water quality and clarity

>inexpensive

The underwater foliage of **SUBMERGED PLANTS** filters unwanted nutrients, improving water quality and clarity. Too many submerged plants, however, can cause wide pH swings. If your pond has fish, plant no more submerged plants than will cover an area about half the size of the pond.

Hornwort
(Ceratophyllum demersum)
- **ZONES 5 TO 11**
- **HEIGHT: TO 10 FEET • WIDTH: 1 FOOT OR MORE**
- **WATER DEPTH: 1 TO 10 FEET**

Looking a little like an underwater juniper, hornwort is a many-branched oxygenator with thick, dense dark green foliage. It grows in a fluffy mat that floats just below the water surface. Because it doesn't produce roots, there's no need for a pot or soil—just place it in the pond. If you want to keep the plant in one spot and at a certain depth, secure it to a brick with a rubber band. Hornwort makes an excellent spawning ground for fish in spring and is somewhat resistant to koi feeding.

Fanwort (Cabomba caroliniana)
- **ZONES 5 TO 11**
- **HEIGHT: TO 6 FEET • WIDTH: 1 FOOT**
- **WATER DEPTH: 1 TO 10 FEET**

A submerged aquatic with delicate and finely cut foliage (dark green above, deep purple underneath), fanwort is winter-hardy, even in cold regions where ice forms on the pond. In summer, it grows long stems that reach to the water surface and sprout a multitude of small white flowers with bright yellow centers. An attractive aquatic in the backyard pond, it has a fluffy structure that is excellent for goldfish spawning.

< 38 >

Foxtail
(Myriophyllum heterophyllum)

- ZONES 3 TO 11
- HEIGHT: TO 6 FEET • WIDTH: 1 FOOT
- WATER DEPTH: 1 TO 10 FEET

A winter-hardy underwater favorite, this plant has thin, wispy leaves that grow from a stout central stem. The foliage is fluffy when submerged, somewhat like a fox's tail, from which it derives its common name. There are several similar species including *M. hippuroides,* and *M. spicata. M. spicata* is often sold, but it is highly invasive. Avoid adding it to your water feature.

Water violet *(Hottonia palustris)*

- ZONES 5 TO 9
- HEIGHT: 18 TO 30 INCHES • WIDTH: 12 TO 20 INCHES
- WATER DEPTH: TO 18 INCHES

Water violet holds its light green foliage above and below the water. As with other oxygenators, the floating leaves offer valuable shade while the submerged ones absorb fish wastes. The real beauty of the water violet is its flower spikes, which rise above the pond's surface in spring with a profusion of small pale lilac flowers. Water violet is suitable for still or moving water.

Anacharis *(Egeria densa)*

- ZONES 8 TO 11
- HEIGHT: 10 FEET • WIDTH 1 FOOT
- WATER DEPTH: 1 FOOT TO 10 FEET

Anacharis has shiny, fleshy bright green leaves that radiate from a central stem, like a feather duster. In summer, its white flowers float on the water surface. Overwinter stem cuttings indoors in an aquarium.

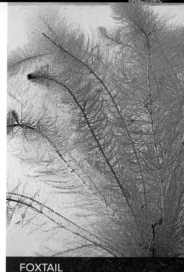

FOXTAIL

WATER VIOLET

< 39 >

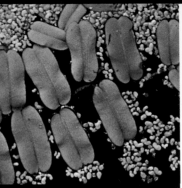

SALVINIA

FAIRY MOSS

FLOATING PLANTS are the ultimate in easy gardening. There's no potting necessary—just place them in the water. Because they sit on the water surface, floaters grow in any depth of water. They are among the best filtrators. They also shade fish from sun and protect them from predators. The stems of some floaters may rise above the water surface; most have an unlimited ability to spread. Too many floaters in a pond, however, can reduce oxygen, which fish need to live. Occasionally thin out the plants to prevent floaters from completely covering the pond's surface.

Salvinia *(Salvinia oblongifolia)*
- **ZONES 10 AND 11**
- **HEIGHT: WATER LEVEL**

Salvinia is a true fern. The species has velvety leaves that grow on a long floating chain. Because it is too aggressive in southern climates, salvinia should be used only in northern areas. It's excellent in containers or small ponds where control is easier. Salvinia is a good food source for small fish. Be sure to thin plants regularly to prevent them from shading the entire pond. Water should be at least 40°F before planting salvinia.

Fairy moss *(Azolla caroliniana)*
- **ZONES 9 AND 11**
- **HEIGHT: WATER LEVEL**

Like salvinia, fairy moss is a true fern. It has fuzzy, finely toothed leaves that are bright green in summer and red in spring and fall. The color and texture of the leaves are excellent in container water gardens and dish gardens. Fairy moss provides cover for fish and other wildlife. Because they grow best when days are long, plants are difficult to carry over inside in winter. Toss dead plants on your compost pile; they fix their own nitrogen and will enrich the pile.

FLOATING PLANT FEATURES

PLANTING DEPTH: just below the surface of the water

LIGHT: sun to part shade

PLANT TYPE: many are perennial; non-hardy plants grow as annuals

>improve water quality and clarity

>add eye-catching texture to the surface of pond

>easy to grow in small containers

< **40** >

Water hyacinth
(Eichhornia crassipes)

• **ZONES 9 TO 11**

• **HEIGHT: TO 1 FOOT**

Known for its lavender flowers and shiny, round, spongy green foliage, this floater filters water so well that it is sometimes grown to treat sewage. Water hyacinth makes an ideal container plant. Drop it in a pot that holds water and add fertilizer. It does best in warm water and won't survive freezing weather. Plant when water is at least 65°F. Treat it like an annual. Note: It is illegal to possess water hyacinth in some states, and federal law prohibits interstate commerce of it.

WATER HYACINTH

Water lettuce (Pistia stratiotes)

• **ZONES 9 TO 11**

• **HEIGHT: 4 TO 12 INCHES**

Water lettuce's spongy, velvety lime-green foliage grows like a rosette from a single crown, resembling a floating head of lettuce. This easy-to-grow plant is at home in the confines of a container and grows equally well in a large pond. Plant water lettuce when water temperature is at least 65°F.

Notes

_____

_____

_____

_____

_____

WATER LETTUCE

_____

_____

_____

_____

_____

< 41 >

'COLORADO'

'HELVOLA'

'REMBRANDT'

HARDY WATER LILIES

HARDY WATER LILY FEATURES	
LIGHT: full sun	
HEIGHT: floating	
WIDTH: to 8', depending on cultivar	
WATER DEPTH: 6–36"	
FLOWERS: buds form and flowers open when pond water is over 65°F.	
ZONES: 3–11	

HARDY WATER LILIES are day-bloomers. They open around 9 a.m. and close around 4 p.m. On dark, cloudy days, they may not open at all. Generally, their flowers rest on the water surface. Hardy water lily cultivars bloom in a wide range of colors, from the darkest reds to the purest whites, with bright pinks and creamy yellows in between. The only colors missing are blues and purples, but hybridizers are developing new plants daily, so expect these colors soon.

Water lilies are often classified by their leaf spread—that is, how much water surface the plant will cover once it is mature. Hardy water lilies can have a spread anywhere from 1 to 8 feet in diameter.

< **42** >

Recommended cultivars

PINK, WHITE, AND YELLOW FLOWERING: 'ALBA' is an easy-to-grow white lily with colorful leaves. 'PEACE' grows well in a wide range of climates, producing pink, white, and yellow flowers. Both are suitable for ponds 6 feet wide or larger. 'HELVOLA' is a dwarf cultivar; it works well in small ponds and container gardens.

PEACH AND SALMON FLOWERING: 'COLORADO' has salmon flowers, with large, pointed petals. 'CYNTHIA ANN' has small peach blossoms suitable for container gardens or small pools.

CHANGEABLE FLOWERS: This group of hardy water lilies has blossoms that open one color and age to a different hue. These are good for small ponds and containers. 'COMANCHE' has flowers that open creamy yellow-apricot and change to peach-pink then to deep reddish-orange.

RED: Most dark red selections are more suitable to northern climates. In warmer areas, red lily petals may "melt" in the summer afternoon sun. 'ALMOST BLACK' has red flowers the color of dark cherry soda. 'FIREBALL' has double blossoms. 'REMBRANDT' is best for large gardens.

How to grow

PLANTING: You can plant hardy water lilies when they are dormant or when they are actively growing. If planting dormant hardy water lilies, wait till the water temperature is at least 50°F.

To plant a dormant or actively growing hardy water lily, fill a pot about two-thirds full of soil. Make a mound in the middle of the pot with a handful of soil. Place the rhizome on the mound, then spread any roots over the top of the soil so they are not under the rhizome. Sprinkle soil over the roots and around the rhizome, adding just enough to cover the rhizome. Do not bury it. It should have no soil on its crown; otherwise, it will have difficulty sprouting new leaves. Water the pot thoroughly, then top it off with pea gravel, again avoiding the crown.

CARE: Overwinter hardy water lilies by moving them to the deepest part of the pond in late fall. Or overwinter by removing foliage, wrapping plants in moist newspaper and then loosely in plastic bags; store in a cool, dark area, such as an old working refrigerator.

Notes

'BLUE BEAUTY'

'ROBERT STRAWN'

'RED FLARE'   'TINA'

TROPICAL WATER LILY FEATURES	
LIGHT: full sun	
HEIGHT: floating	
SPREAD: to 8', depending on cultivar	
WATER DEPTH: 24–36"	
FLOWERS: buds form and flowers open when pond water is warmer than 65°F.	
ZONES: 10 and 11	

WATER LILIES from tropical climates exude an almost intoxicating fragrance. These prized water garden bloomers flower much more profusely than hardy water lilies. The most common color is blue, but they also come in lavender and purple, as well as pink, yellow, and white. Some are small plants suitable for container water gardens. Others can grow more than 8 feet in diameter in a season. One leaf alone may measure more than 2 feet wide. The foliage is often mottled in purple or brown.

Tropical water lilies require special winter care, but their profuse blossoms and sweet fragrance make the fall and winter chores a small price to pay for beautiful flowers.

< **44** >

Recommended cultivars

'ROBERT STRAWN' has lilac-colored petals and a bright yellow center. 'TINA' has purple-blue flowers and is a good water lily for both container gardens and large ponds. 'FLORIDA STAR' has large white star-shaped flowers with yellow centers; it is best for large ponds.

Some tropical water lilies are night-bloomers, opening after the sun sets and staying open until late the next morning. Notable night-bloomers include 'RED FLARE', with rose-pink flowers and dark red foliage, and 'MRS. GEORGE C. HITCHCOCK', with clear pink flowers.

How to grow

PLANTING: Plant tropical water lilies when the water temperature reaches 70°F. Most cultivars will require locations with full sun, but a few can tolerate part shade.

Tropical water lilies require a little detective work to plant at the right depth. Examine the lily's stems, starting at the base. Look for the point where the stem changes color from light to dark. This is the point from which the leaf emerged from the soil. When you plant the lily, the topping-off material (gravel) must be even with this point.

It's important that the main growing crown of a tropical be planted at just the right depth. If it is planted too deeply—especially on a night-blooming cultivar—it will usually stop growing in order to make new plants, taking energy from the main crown. You will eventually have more new plants, but they will be smaller, and by the time they reach the size at which they will bloom well, it may be too late in the season for them to set flowers.

The general planting procedure is the same as for hardy water lilies (see page 43). Hardy and tropical water lily leaves are extremely buoyant. After potting them up, keep plants just 4 to 6 inches below the water surface until their roots have a firm grip on the soil—usually three to four days—to help reduce buoyancy.

CARE: Overwinter tropical water lilies by lifting the potted plants out of the water and storing them in a cool location in moist sand until spring.

Notes

< 45 >

LOTUS *(Nelumbo* species)

LOTUS BLOSSOM

'CHARLES THOMAS'

'ROSEA PLENA'

'CHAWAN BASU'

LOTUS FEATURES	
LIGHT: full sun	
HEIGHT: 6–48", depending on cultivar	
SPREAD: unlimited	
WATER DEPTH: moist to 12"; some varieties can tolerate depths to 36" deep	
FLOWERS: buds form and open after several weeks of 80° weather. They will bloom for 6 to 8 weeks.	
ZONES: 4–11	

Large exotic blossoms in pink, white, and yellow rise above the bright green, round leaves of **LOTUS** in early summer in the South and in midsummer in the North. These fragrant plants range from 6-inch-tall miniature varieties to large varieties that grow 4 feet or more above the water. After blooming for six to eight weeks, the flowers form attractive seedpods that can be used in dried or fresh arrangements.

Lotuses are not a tropical plant; they simply love hot weather, preferring warm soil and water temperatures. Their fragrance, which varies from heady and fruity to mild, is most pronounced in hot, humid conditions.

< 46 >

Recommended cultivars

'ROSEA PLENA' grows has large peony-like rose-pink flowers on 5- to 7-foot-tall stems. 'CHAWAN BASU' has creamy-white flower petals edged with dark pink and grows 2 to 3 feet tall. 'PURE JADE' is a white-flowering, miniature lotus that grows 1 to 2 feet tall. 'RED CHILDREN', another miniature lotus, has light pink flowers. 'BEN GIBSON', a red-tipped pink double lotus, stands 3 to 4 feet tall. The fragrant single blossoms of 'CHARLES THOMAS' bloom pink and fade to lavender; plants grow 3 to 4 feet tall. 'SHARON' has dark pink, semidouble flowers with yellow in the center.

Bowl lotuses, often called teacup lotuses, are like standard lotuses in all respects except for their size. They grow to no more than 2 feet in height, some only 4 inches tall—perfect for tabletop ponds. Red-flowering 'WELCOMING' and 'RED BALL' and pink 'SHINING SUNGLOW' grow to a foot or so tall.

How to grow

PLANTING: Lotuses revel in warm water and humid conditions and do not begin growing in spring until the water temperature reaches 60°F. Plant large lotuses in pots that are 2 to 3 feet in diameter and a foot or more tall. Small lotuses can be planted in smaller pots. These plants grow best in clay soil. Place potted, sun-loving lotus in an area that receives at least six hours of sunlight each day. The pot should be about 6 inches below the water surface.

CARE: Lotuses are heavy feeders. Feed them regularly throughout summer, especially when they are in bloom. When feeding lotus, follow the directions provided by the plant food manufacturer. Overwinter lotuses in the pond, even in cold climates. Cut the summer foliage back to the water surface after leaves have died and turned brown. Put the pot in a part of the pond where ice and frost will not reach the tubers.

Divide lotuses in early spring before they have sprouted leaves. Remove the tubers from the container and gently rinse away the soil. Using scissors or a sharp knife cut the tuber into divisions that contain at least one growing tip and a section of tuber.

Notes

< 47 >

MARGINAL PLANTS grow at the edge, or margin, of the pond where the water is shallow. Some marginals grow in moist or wet soil; others grow in submerged soil—from a few inches to about 2 feet deep. Many marginals will also adapt to the perennial garden. Marginals can be taller than 6 feet or less than 2 inches. Marginals' chief function is decorative, adding color, texture, and form to the design. They're also an important transitional element between the pond and the surrounding landscape.

Cattail *(Typha* species)

Easy-to-grow **CATTAILS** are common in freshwater marshes, where they colonize wide areas with stiff running rhizomes. They thrive in water over their crowns and provide a habitat for amphibians and fish. Their grasslike foliage serves as a nesting place for many species of wild birds, and muskrats often eat their roots. Height ranges from 6 inches in dwarf forms to more than 12 feet in giant varieties.

COMMON CATTAIL

Recommended cultivars

COMMON CATTAIL *(Typha latifolia)* is the standard cattail seen in ditches and wetlands. It is excellent for water filtration, but grows rapidly and can be invasive. **GRACEFUL CATTAIL** *(T. angustifolia)* is narrow-leaved with foliage that arches and sways in the wind. This elegant variety is suitable for most ponds and large container water gardens.

How to grow

PLANTING: In the pond, plant cattail in a container and submerge it to 4 inches below the water surface or grow cattail in soil at the edge of the pond.

CARE: Plants overwinter well in cool water and withstand freezing temperatures. Divide plants as needed to control size.

MARGINAL PLANT FEATURES
LIGHT: full sun to part shade
HEIGHT: 6" to more than 12', depending on cultivar
WIDTH: unlimited
WATER DEPTH: moist soil to 4" of water
FLOWERS: long catkins that turn brown as they mature
ZONES: 3–11

Notes

_____

_____

_____

_____

_____

< 48 >

Eye-catching **CYPERUS** plants hold ornamental mop-top heads aloft like umbrellas on 2- to 12-foot-tall stems. They're functional too, filtering excess nutrients from the water. Flowers are small and green and turn tawny brown as the seeds develop. There's a cyperus—from very large to very small—for every pond.

Recommended cultivars

UMBRELLA GRASS *(C. alternifolius)* is the most commonly sold species. Its top leaf sprout can grow up to 2 feet in diameter, forming the characteristic umbrella shape. Fast-growing umbrella grass usually needs dividing every few years to keep the center from becoming woody and empty of foliage.

DWARF UMBRELLA GRASS *(C. alternifolius* 'Nanus') is a compact plant with long, umbrellalike fronds; it's hardy in Zones 9 to 11 and grows 2 feet tall.

PAPYRUS *(C. papyrus)* and **MEXICAN PAPYRUS** *(C. giganteus)* are favorites of many water gardeners. Papyrus is stunning, with its 10-inch ball of long green threads; Mexican papyrus has 20-inch spheres of wiry foliage on stiff, erect, nonarching stems. Both are hardy in Zones 8 to 11 and grow in moist soil to 12-inch-deep water. They reach 5 to 12 feet tall and spread 4 to 5 feet wide.

How to grow

PLANTING: Plant cyperus in a pot and place it below the water surface as directed by the plant tag; depth varies with the species. Where cyperus is hardy, you can plant it in soil beside the pond.

CARE: All species are heavy feeders and should be fed at least once a month. Only a few species are hardy in cold regions, but plants can be overwintered in a moist location where temperatures hover around 60°F.

Notes

_____

_____

_____

_____

< 49 >

PAPYRUS

CYPERUS FEATURES
LIGHT: sun to part shade
HEIGHT: 2–12', depending on cultivar
SPREAD: 2–5'
WATER DEPTH: varies with species
FLOWERS: true flowers are small; the umbrellas, which you might assume are flowers, are actually leaves
ZONES: 7–11

HIBISCUS

HIBISCUS has brightly colored, dinner-plate-size flowers. This attention-grabber blooms continuously for several weeks in midsummer and attracts hummingbirds and butterflies. It is also easy to grow in a perennial border that has moist soil.

Recommended cultivars

WATER HIBISCUS *(H. moscheutos palustris)* is a true aquatic, thriving in wet soil to flowing water. It branches freely and has pink rosy-throated flowers. Plants tolerate seasonal flooding up to 2 feet deep.

SWAMP MALLOW *(H. moscheutos)* has stunning, 10- to 12-inch flowers ranging from white to deep red. It is usually larger-flowering and bushier than water hibiscus but not as water tolerant.

'BLUE DANUBE' has large, pristine white flowers. **'COPPER KING'** has red cutleaf foliage and red or pink 12-inch-wide blooms. Both plants bloom all summer.

How to grow

PLANTING: Place potted hibiscus 6 inches below the water surface, or plant hibiscus in moist soil at the pond edge.

CARE: In cold climates hibiscus may die back to the crown in winter. It is slow to emerge in spring. In fall, mark where it is planted to remind you where it is before it emerges in late spring or early summer.

Notes

HIBISCUS FEATURES
LIGHT: sun to part shade
HEIGHT: 4–6'
SPREAD: 2–4'
WATER DEPTH: moist soil to 6" deep water
FLOWERS: showy bright, colored flowers
ZONES: 5–11

< 50 >

HOUTTUYNIA *(Houttuynia cordata* 'Chameleon')

'CHAMELEON' HOUTTUYNIA leaves are splashed with red, cream, and green to create a variegated pattern. The heart-shaped leaves form a dense mat and have a spicy fragrance when crushed. In fall they turn maroon-purple.

'Chameleon' houttuynias are excellent ground covers. Grow them under upright stalks of iris or butterfly weed. A good plant for the edge of the pond, 'Chameleon' thrives in moist soil.

This marginal grows so well that it can become invasive. Confine its roots by planting it in a pot.

Recommended cultivars

Other houttuynia cultivars include **'VARIEGATA'** which has green and white leaves. **'FLORE PLENO'** has green leaves and double white blooms that resemble rosebuds.

How to grow

PLANTING: Plant houttuynia in a pot. Place the pot in soil at the edge of the pond or in water up to 1 inch deep.

CARE: Houttuynia is a tender plant; overwinter it by submerging it in the deepest part of the pond. Or take it inside and enjoy it as a houseplant during winter.

Notes

_____
_____
_____
_____
_____
_____
_____
_____
_____
_____

HOUTTUYNIA

HOUTTUYNIA FEATURES
LIGHT: sun to shade
HEIGHT: 6–8"
SPREAD: running
WATER DEPTH: moist soil to 1" of water
FLOWERS: true flowers are white and small; variegated foliage is the plant's notable trait
ZONES: 5–11

< 51 >

IRIS (*Iris* species)

YELLOW FLAG IRIS

SIBERIAN IRIS | 'QUEEN OF VIOLETS'

FEATURES	
LIGHT: sun to part shade	
HEIGHT: 2'–4'	
WIDTH: 1–2½'	
WATER DEPTH: moist soil to 3–6" deep water	
FLOWERS: purple, yellow, white, and orange-hued flowers rise gracefully above swordlike foliage	
ZONES: 3–9	

In spring, elegant flowers in a rainbow of colors decorate **IRIS**. Different types of iris grow in and near the pond. True water irises include yellow flag (*I. pseudacorus*), blue flag (*I. versicolor*), southern blue flag (*I. hexagona*), and rabbit-ear iris (*I. laevigata*). These species grow best with water over their crowns throughout the year, even in fall and winter. Other irises, such as Japanese iris (*I. ensata*), Siberian iris (*I. sibirica*), and Rocky Mountain iris (*I. missouriensis*), tolerate wet soil for part of the growing season but prefer drier conditions.

< 52 >

Recommended cultivars

Yellow flag iris owes its name to its bright yellow flowers that appear in early spring. It is hardy in Zones 5 to 8. Growing as tall as 4 feet, yellow flag iris is suitable for larger ponds. 'SULPHUR QUEEN' has pale yellow flowers, while 'GOLDEN QUEEN' is a richer hue. 'BERLIN TIGER' has yellow flowers veined with brown.

Both blue flag and southern blue flag have light blue flowers in midspring, and their blue-green sword-shaped leaves take on a tinge of dark red from the base to the tips. These iris are hardy in Zones 3 to 9. Southern blue flag cultivars include 'CANDY STRIPER', with white flowers veined in red. If you live in a northern climate, try southern blue flag cultivars 'POND LILAC DREAM', with lavender-pink blooms with darker colored veining and creamy-yellow marks down the center of the petal, and 'DOTTIE'S DOUBLE', a double-petaled variety with lavender veins.

Japanese water iris (*I. laevigata*) often grows in masses along stream banks. 'QUEEN OF VIOLETS' has long-lasting purple flowers.

Siberian irises work well in the bog garden or in moist areas of the perennial garden and are hardy in Zones 4 to 9. Flowers of 'CORONATION ANTHEM' are indigo blue, shading to white toward their center. 'SHAKER'S PRAYER' is soft periwinkle-blue freckled with white.

How to grow

PLANTING: Plant irises in spring immediately after flowering. Set them so the top of their rhizome, or root, is less than 1 inch below the surface of the soil. Plants that don't flower might be planted too deeply.

CARE: Water garden irises need minimal attention through the summer but are subject to a few maladies, such as thrips, nematodes, and rhizome rot. Combat pests by sheltering plants from wind and hot afternoon sun, and feed them monthly while they are growing. Mulch plants heavily in late summer or early fall to help them withstand the winter cold. Divide crowded clumps in spring after they finish flowering and replant immediately.

Notes

< 53 >

RUSH (*Juncus* species)

CORKSCREW RUSH

The stately, upright foliage of **RUSH** is a useful element in the water garden. Most rushes are noted for their long spiked stems, which are usually dark green but can be light blue. Foliage is stiff and hollow.

Grow rush as a background or screen plant or pair it with a collection of floating plants for contrast. Rush also provides important shelter for fish, fowl, and insects.

In many climates rushes are evergreen. Plants may be grown in the perennial border as long as they are given adequate moisture.

Recommended cultivars

SOFT RUSH (*J. effusus*) has stiff spines of green foliage. It can retain its color all year, even in cold climates. **CORKSCREW RUSH** (*J. effusus* 'Spiralis') has tightly coiled foliage, which is excellent in fresh or dried floral arrangements. **'GOLD STRIKE'** has dark green leaves accented with gold stripes along their length. **BLUE RUSH** (*J. inflexus*) has baby-blue foliage that resembles that of blue fescue. It grows in full sun and takes moist soil to 2-inch-deep water. It is hardy to Zone 4.

How to grow

PLANTING: Place potted plants in or beside the water garden in spring.

CARE: Most rushes are cold-tolerant and can be overwintered in the pond. Keep rush tidy by cutting it back to the ground in early spring to remove older, tattered growth. Divide rushes in spring with a sharp spade when plants become crowded.

Notes

RUSH FEATURES
LIGHT: sun to part shade
HEIGHT: 2–3'
SPREAD: 2'
WATER DEPTH: moist soil to 4" deep
FLOWERS: flowers appear as brown tassels that droop from near or at the tip of the leaves; grown primarily for foliage
ZONES: 4–9

< 54 >

SWEET FLAGS have a neat, clean appearance. They grow tall and upright and may be green or variegated. Their roots run freely and form small clumps. Hardy and foolproof, they add textural interest to a pond. Plant them with flowering plants such as iris, water lilies, lotus, and cannas.

Recommended cultivars

Graceful 'OGON' JAPANESE SWEET FLAG *(A. gramineus)* has light green foliage with bright yellow stripes. It is evergreen in most regions.

How to grow

PLANTING: In spring or fall, plant sweet flag in shallow water or in moist soil in the garden. Plants do well in sun or shade.

CARE: Sweet flags need constantly moist soil; their leaf tips will burn when underwatered. Most types tolerate seasonal flooding; once mature, they can handle several inches of water over the crown. Japanese sweet flag, however, can't take water over its crown for more than a few days.

SWEET FLAG

All sweet flags can overwinter in the pond or in a mulched perennial border. Make sure they're well watered before soil freezes. Where soil doesn't freeze, don't let them dry out. Divide crowded plants anytime from spring through fall.

Smaller forms are prone to spider mites. Larger selections may develop a fungus that causes black spot and can kill foliage. Clean up dead foliage in autumn and remove spotted leaves to prevent disease spread.

Notes

_____

_____

_____

_____

_____

_____

SWEET FLAG FEATURES
LIGHT: sun to part shade
HEIGHT: 8–36"
SPREAD: to 18" wide, depending on cultivar
WATER DEPTH: moist soil to 2–6" of water
FLOWERS: true flowers are small and insignificant; grown primarily for its stiff, upright leaves
ZONES: 4–11

< 55 >

TARO *(Colocasia esculenta)*

TARO, with its massive foliage and graceful habit, is ideal for container water gardens as well as full-size ponds. Also called elephant-ear, this bold plant thrives in hot, humid weather and will produce larger leaves if you protect it from the afternoon sun. The petiole, or leaf stalk, comes in many beautiful colors, so locate the plants to show them off.

'BLACK MAGIC' TARO

TARO FEATURES
LIGHT: sun to part shade
HEIGHT: 2–6'
SPREAD: 2–4'
WATER DEPTH: moist soil to 6" deep water
FLOWERS: true flowers are small and insignificant; grown for its large, arrow-shaped leaves
ZONES: 9–11

Recommended cultivars

'BLACK MAGIC' taro has very dark, black-purple leaves and stems. 'METALLICA' is particularly elegant, with deep purple stems and large velvety, blue-green leaves. 'CHICAGO HARLEQUIN' has stems striped in purple and white and large decorative leaves veined in purple. 'FORTANESII' has leaves with dark red to purple stalks and veins.

GIANT TARO *(Alocasia macrorrhiza)* looks similar to elephant's ear. Its leaves are a little narrower and more arrow-shaped. They are truly gigantic—up to 6 feet long—and have an upright habit. Giant taro tolerates mild frost. In Zones 9 and warmer, plants will develop a woody trunk. 'NEW GUINEA GOLD' has gold-speckled green leaves.

How to grow

PLANTING: Taro grows from a large tuber. Plant the tuber 6 inches deep in a large pot and place it in the pond in spring.

CARE: A heavy feeder, taro benefits from monthly feeding. Overwinter plants indoors by keeping the pots in saucers of water in a warm, sunny room. Or let the foliage die back after a frost, dig up the corms, and store them until spring in coarse vermiculite in a sealed container or in a cool (but frost-free), dark spot.

Notes

_____

_____

_____

_____

WATER CANNA *(Canna* species)

Long-lasting, bright-hued flowers are the hallmark of **CANNAS**. Their vibrant red, orange, and yellow flowers appear in midsummer and last until frost. Canna foliage is large, long, and tropical looking, and can be bright green, blue-green, dark purple, crimson, or striped in yellow, white, or red.

Plant cannas near the edge of the pond to frame a view. Or use them as a tropical focal point. Their long-lasting flowers make canna an excellent choice for the water garden.

Recommended cultivars

TRUE WATER CANNAS *(C. glauca* and *C. flaccida)* grow well in saturated soil with water over their crowns. Other cannas are land lovers but will adapt to waterlogged soil. Examples of terrestrial cannas include 'AUSTRALIA' with shiny deep burgundy foliage and red-orange flowers; 'BENGAL TIGER' with yellow-and-white-striped leaves; and 'ORCHID' which has pink flowers with yellow throats.

How to grow

PLANTING: Plant canna rhizomes in moist soil or in pots to submerge in the water garden in spring. Set rhizomes so their eyes, or growing points, face up; cover them with 2 inches of soil.

CARE: Cannas cannot withstand a freeze. In cold regions, lift rhizomes and store indoors in winter. In warm regions, cannas can be left in the ground year-round. Divide large clumps every two to three years in spring.

Aphids and Japanese beetles will eat the foliage in summer.

Notes

_____

_____

_____

_____

_____

_____

WATER CANNA

WATER CANNA FEATURES
LIGHT: sun to part shade
HEIGHT: 3–10', depending on cultivar
SPREAD: 2–3'
WATER DEPTH: moist soil to 10–12" deep
FLOWERS: striking, long-lasting red, yellow, or orange blossoms
ZONES: 9–11

< 57 >

Potting Up a Water Plant

While plants in natural ponds root in the mud on the bottom of the pond, those in garden ponds (except floaters) thrive in pots. Plant most water garden plants in the same way as terrestrial plants, then set them gently in the pool. You can introduce them into the pond immediately after filling it, following the precautions on page 34.

❶ **GATHER YOUR SUPPLIES.** You'll need high-quality potting soil formulated for water gardens. It should not contain peat or perlite, which will float out of the pot. Also avoid potting soil that contains fertilizer.

You'll also need containers in which to pot the plants. Black plastic pots make great containers for pond plants. Although containers made specifically for water planting are available, the plastic pots you get at the nursery work just as well. Pot size should be matched to the size and type of plant. Because most water plants grow only in the top 10 to 12 inches of soil, that's as deep as the container needs to be.

Also pick up pea gravel or dark gravel to top the containers and a variety of risers, such as exterior bricks or black plastic storage boxes, to set the plants on and position them at the right depth in the pond.

REMOVE THE PLANT from its original container. Partially fill the new pot with soil. Mix in a slow-release water garden plant food into the soil, following label recommendations. Gently position the plant on top. ❷ If planting a hardy water lily, set its root ball at the edge of the pot. ❸ Plant tropical water lilies in the center of the container. Make sure the plant is at the same level it was in its original container.

< 58 >

TOP THE ROOTS WITH SOIL, filling the pot to a half inch below the rim. Pinch off any damaged or yellow leaves. Water the pot thoroughly to eliminate air pockets. Top off the container with more soil if needed.

4 SPREAD A LAYER OF PEA GRAVEL or dark gravel on top of the soil to keep it from floating out of the container and to help it blend into the background of the pond bottom.

5 POSITION THE PLANT IN THE POND at the correct level. To raise a plant, stack a few weathered bricks underneath it or put the pot on a black plastic storage crate. Be careful, pots can be heavy; enlist a friend to help you move the pots into the pond. You may need to get into the water to position some plants.

When fall rolls around, gardeners in cold climates will have to remove nonhardy water garden plants and move the hardy species to the deep zone of the pond.

Fertilizer Note
Once established, water garden plants benefit from fertilizing. But regular fertilizers can be toxic to fish and can encourage algae. Use aquatic fertilizer instead; it's sold as large pellets, which you push into the soil. Aquatic fertilizer is available at garden centers or through mail-order companies.

Fish bring color and movement to your water garden. They also keep the mosquito population in check. Stocking a pond requires careful planning. Follow these guidelines for adding fish to your outdoor oasis.

START WITH A FEW FISH, then gradually add more. Maintain a healthy pond ecosystem by providing ample space for each fish. Goldfish require at least 5 gallons of water per inch of fish. They are easy to care for and thrive in ponds of all sizes, small and large. Koi, which require at least 10 gallons of water per inch of fish, are best in large ponds.

NEUTRALIZE POND WATER before introducing fish. Fish can't tolerate the chemicals commonly found in municipal water supplies. Follow the directions on page 34 to remove harmful chemicals from your pond.

ALLOW FISH TO ACCLIMATIZE TO THE WATER before releasing them into the pond. Float the bag containing the new fish in the pond until the water in the bag is within 2°F of the temperature of the water in the pond. Roll down the top of the bag and splash in some of the pond water. Once the water has warmed, add the fish to the pond, but don't add the water from the bag.

FEED YOUR FISH AT THE SAME TIME EVERY DAY and you'll soon see them eagerly awaiting you in the pond. Give them as much as they'll eat in 10 minutes or so. Use floating pellets or flakes so that when they're done feeding, you can skim leftover food from the pond. Uneaten fish food will decompose and foul the water.

KEEP THE FISH POPULATION IN CHECK. Plants are favorite snacks of koi and some other fish. Large koi and an overpopulation of fish will overturn pots and can destroy plants. If possible, remove some of the fish from the pond and find a home for them with other water gardeners. Maintain healthy plants and fish by stocking your pond with small goldfish less than 10 inches long.

OVERWINTER FISH IN PONDS THAT DO NOT FREEZE TO THE BOTTOM. Goldfish and koi overwinter well in ponds equipped with a deicer, which maintains an opening on the icy surface of the pond. The fish will hibernate at the bottom of the pond. Tropical fish must be overwintered indoors when the water dips below 70°F.

< 60 >

❶ Common goldfish

Usually orange-red, common goldfish are easy to care for in a small pond. Most grow less than 10 inches long, are easily bred, and may live for 10 years or more. They prefer a weedy pond with a muddy bottom. Common goldfish are hardy. They will tolerate water as cool as 39°F and as warm as 95°F, though not for long periods at either extreme.

❷ Koi

Though choice koi are costly, not all koi are expensive. They grow to about 2 feet long; are hearty eaters, especially of plants; and need a large pond with a good filtration system to dispose of their considerable waste. They can be boisterous enough to knock over pots. Koi breed easily. They prefer cool water temperatures, from 39°F to 68°F.

❸ Red comet

A relatively new type of goldfish, red comets boast elegantly long fins and tail. Red comets are hardy, tolerating water as cool as 39°F and as warm as 95°F, but not for long periods at either extreme.

❹ Shubunkins

Often called calico goldfish, shubunkins are popular and easy to care for. They come in many colors, including blue. Shubunkins grow to 10 inches and are hardy, tolerating temperatures between 39°F and 85°F.

< 62 >

Tabletop Water Feature

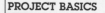

PROJECT BASICS

TIME: 2 hours

SKILL: easy

MATERIALS:

- a watertight container
- floating plants
- miniature water lily or other plants
- garden soil or aquatic planting mix
- pea gravel
- small stones

Dip into water gardening in a small way by setting up a tabletop design. You can use many of the same plants you would in a larger garden; in fact, some that become invasive in a pond behave better in the restricted space of a container.

Choose any container that does not have drainage holes in the bottom. Float plants in water. Or treat them as if they were marginal or bog plants, and grow them in a layer of soil topped with a layer of pea gravel. Then fill the container with water and keep the soil wet at all times.

< 64 >

❶ First, select a watertight container. Any container will do, even a simple serving bowl like the one here works well. Place a 1- to 2-inch layer of flat stones, such as river rock, on the bottom of the container. These stones will serve as a filter, collecting plant debris.

❷ Fill the basin with water to within 1 inch of the rim. The water will evaporate rapidly when the tabletop garden is outdoors. Plan to top off the water every couple of days.

❸ Plant the basin with a variety of water plants. You can use all floating plants as we did here. Water lettuce, pictured, grows rapidly and has a pleasing texture. Combine it with white-flowered water snowflake for an attractive mix or with fairy moss or foxtail for good textural contrast.

Potted water plants, such as miniature water lilies are also good candidates for a tabletop water garden. Pour 3 to 4 inches of garden soil or a commercial aquatic planting mix into the container. Plant the water lily in the soil, then top with pea gravel. Add water to within an inch of the rim.

❹ Place your tabletop water garden in full sun or part shade. Keep a close watch on the water level and fill the basin as it evaporates. In a few weeks the plants will cover the water surface.

Maintain a healthy ecosystem by thinning out the vigorous growers every few weeks. Floating plants, such as water lettuce, water hyacinth, and duckweed, require regular thinning or they will smother nearby plants.

In fall, move your tabletop garden indoors. Although most water plants will not bloom in the subdued indoor light, the sculptural quality of their leaves often provides enough interest to take the place of blooms.

< 65 >

Simple Bell Fountain

PROJECT BASICS

TIME: 4 hours

SKILL: easy

MATERIALS:

- a preformed pond liner
- sand
- pump
- fiberglass
- window screening
- a fountain head
- heavy-duty resin grate
- cinder block
- rocks
- rigid PVC pipe (equal in length to the span from the fountain site to the nearest electrical outlet)
- river rock
- zip ties
- hose clamps

Enjoy the gentle sound of cascading water with this easy-to-install in-ground pool and fountain. Perfect near a deck or patio, this fountain will add water music to your dining area.

Personalize your fountain by using any fountain head you like. We used a bell-shaped fountain head here, but the step-by-step process is the same for any fountain head you choose. In fact, if you would like to turn a pretty urn or other decorative object into a fountain, simply run the vinyl tubing through the urn rather than attaching a fountain head. See examples of easy in-ground pool and fountain projects on the following pages.

< 66 >

❶ Gather supplies and tools. Besides those listed in the materials box under Project Basics on the previous page, you'll need a shovel, level, tape measure, screwdriver, pliers, jigsaw, and pruners or scissors.

❷ Dig a hole slightly larger than the pond liner and 1 inch deeper. To avoid compacting nearby soil as you work, stand on scrap pieces of wood while excavating the pond. Preformed liners should fit snugly in the excavated space. Check every so often to ensure the fit.

For easy clean-up have a tarp or wheelbarrow nearby in which to toss the excavated soil. Spread 1 to 2 inches of sand in the bottom of the hole.

❸ Check that the liner sits level in the hole, taking plenty of time to ensure that the liner is absolutely level. A water feature that is not level will slowly leak water and require constant topping off.

❹ Backfill around the liner with fine soil, checking the level as you work. Occasionally tamp the backfill with the shovel handle to firm the soil and eliminate air pockets.

continued on page 68>>

Simple Bell Fountain

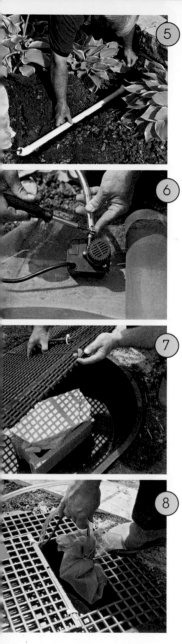

<<continued from page 67

5 Dig a 2-inch-deep trench from the electrical outlet to the liner. Thread the pump cord through the PVC pipe, place the pipe in the trench, and cover with soil.

Note: For safety be sure the outlet you are using has a ground fault circuit interrupter (GFCI) to protect against electrical shock.

6 Attach the fountain head to the pump, or if using an urn, attach vinyl tubing to the pump with a hose clamp. Wrap fiberglass window screening around the pump as a filter.

7 Place cinder blocks and rocks in the bottom of the liner. Prepare the grate by cutting a door in its center with a jigsaw. The door should be only large enough to place the pump in the liner and allow the fountain head to rise above the grate. Leave the door off when using a fountain head; attach the door to the grate with zip ties when setting up an urn fountain. Place the grate over the liner.

8 Lower the pump into the reservoir and onto the cinder blocks. Adjust the height of the blocks to achieve the desired fountain height. Fill the liner, then test the pump, adjusting water flow to prevent excessive splashing. For an urn fountain, close the door with the tubing snaking out through the grate.

Top the grate with a layer of river rock and fill the liner with water. Plug in the pump and enjoy your fountain.

Notes

_____

_____

_____

_____

< 68 >

PROJECT BASICS

TIME: 4 hours

SKILL: easy

MATERIALS:
- 13' of 1" copper pipe
- three 1" copper tees
- two 1" copper elbows
- four two-hole metal pipe straps
- pump
- 6' of ⅝" vinyl tubing
- waterproof adhesive
- foam sealant
- planter
- 3 copper wall plaques
- copper wire

A perfect focal point or noise buffer, this large copper fountain will drown out nearby traffic noise while adding beauty to your porch, patio, or deck.

Constructed with copper tubing, which is available at local home improvement stores, the fountain is powered by a small pump. You can add a personal touch to the fountain by hanging unique wall plaques, tin ceiling tiles, or other ornaments from the top of the fountain with copper wire. For longevity, remove water from the fountain and store it in a covered place during winter.

< 70 >

❶ Begin by cutting the copper pipe to size. You  will need: four 3-inch pieces for the feet; one 5-foot piece for the left leg; one 2-inch piece and one 56-inch piece for the right leg; and one 18-inch piece for the bridge.

Put together the left leg: Insert two 3-inch pieces into a copper tee, one on each side. This forms the foot for the leg. Next, insert the 5-foot piece into the top hole of the tee.

❷ Create a tubing support: Cut a 6-foot-long  piece of vinyl tubing. Thread it through the side hole of a copper tee and out the top, leaving a 6-inch tail.

Make the right leg: Thread the long end of the tubing through the 56-inch copper pipe. Firmly press this pipe into the tubing support as in ❷. Next, make a foot for the leg, inserting two 3-inch copper pipes into either side of a tee.  Then insert a 2-inch copper pipe in the top hole of the tee. Attach this unit to the open end of the tubing support.

❸ Create a bridge from which the water flows by drilling 10 holes across the 18-inch copper pipe. Evenly space the holes, starting 2 inches in from either end. Squirt foam sealant into the center of a copper elbow (this prevents water from flowing down the leg rather than out the holes). Allow the sealant to dry according to directions, then attach it to the top of the left leg.

Next, assemble the fountain by joining all parts in this order: left leg, blocked elbow, bridge, open elbow, then right leg.

Place the fountain in the planter and mark the location of the feet. Remove the fountain; take off the feet. Glue both feet to the planter; for added support, glue metal pipe straps over them. Reposition the fountain on the feet, place the pump in the bottom of the planter and attach it to the 6-inch vinyl tubing tail; run the electrical cord over the side of the planter. Fill the planter with water and plug in the pump. Check the water flow and make adjustments as needed. Hang wall plaques or other decorative items from the bridge to glitter in the flowing water.

< 71 >

Wall Fountain

PROJECT BASICS

TIME: 2 hours

SKILL: easy

MATERIALS:

- spout ornament
- basin, pot, or trough
- flexible tubing
- pencil
- pump
- drill
- masonry or wood bits and screws
- plumber's putty

Add sound and movement to a forlorn wall or quiet corner of your outdoor living area with a preassembled easy-to-install fountain kit. A variety of kits are commercially available and take just a few minutes to put together. Some kits are complex or heavy and may require a second set of hands in order to put them together.

< **72** >

1 Choose a location for your fountain that is sturdy enough to safely bear all the necessary components: the spout, the water-filled basin (especially if the basin attaches to a wall), the tubing, and the pump.

To mount the spout for a wall fountain, use a pencil to mark the location where a hole should be drilled for the spout. Using a masonry or wood bit, drill a pilot hole in the wall and insert a screw and hang the spout.

Next, position the basin so that when installation is finished, it will catch the water that falls from the spout. Place the pump in the basin. Run the tubing from the pump through the back of the spout.

2 Check the alignment of the basin beneath the spout and make sure it is level and secure, in order to avoid damage to your home and water loss from the basin. To minimize the appearance of the cord, drill a hole through the side of the basin that will sit against the wall. The hole needs to be large enough for the plug end to pass through. It should also be 1 or more inches above the top of the pump so that if water happens to leak out the hole, the pump will remain submerged and not run dry. Thread the cord through the hole. Seal around the cord with plumber's putty.

3 Run the pump's electrical cord to a nearby GFCI outlet. Fill the basin with water, install the pump, and turn it on. Check to be sure that water from the spout is pouring at the desired volume and falling into the basin in the correct position. Adjust the flow as needed.

< **73** >

PROJECT BASICS

TIME: 2 days

SKILL: moderate to advanced

MATERIALS:
- underlayment
- flexible liner
- stones in a variety of sizes; from river rock to small boulders
- pump
- plastic tubing
- pond liner adhesive

A gentle slope is a perfect location for a small stream with a series of tiny pools. With the help of a pump and strategically buried plastic tubing, water is transported from the catch basin at the bottom of the stream back up to its head where it then begins its trickling descent again.

Make your stream look like it has always been in your backyard by edging it with an assortment of native stones. Use small, medium, and large stones for a natural effect. Finish the stream by surrounding it with easy-care perennial plants and small shrubs.

< **74** >

❶ The type of soil in your garden and the stream's length will determine how easy it is to build a stream. Plan to spend at least four to eight hours excavating by hand a 150-foot-long course like this one. If you're building a large stream, you might want to consider renting a skid steer loader to ease the job.

Begin by marking the watercourse with stakes. For a natural appearance let the stream meander as it moves down the hill. Also vary the stream's width. Every couple of feet, denote flat "steps," which will pool water and slow its progress downhill. At the end of the stream, mark a catch basin to collect the water before it is pumped back to the top of the stream.

Dig the stream runs 5 to 6 inches deep, using the excavated soil to mound up the sides of the stream or to fill low spots elsewhere on your property. At the steps where the water will pool, dig flat areas 5 inches below the surrounding grade. The catch basin can be shallow or deep enough to double as a water garden. For a shallow basin, dig an 18-inch-deep well for the pump at the lowest point on the stream. At this location, the pump provides maximum water circulation and aeration. If the catch basin will also act as a water garden, excavate to the appropriate depth for your region.

❷ Tamp the soil in the streambed to prevent it from settling after the stream is finished. Remove sharp objects in the streambed as you work. Spread underlayment over the streambed, keeping an eye out for any sharp objects you may have missed. Trim the underlayment as needed to cover all parts of the stream.

❸ Next install the flexible liner. This step can be challenging to do over a large space such as a

continued on page 76>>

< 75 >

<<continued from page 75

stream. Enlist the help of a friend. Use boulders to hold the liner in place as you drape the liner over the meandering course.

4 The unique size and shape of the catch basin may require you to line it separately from the rest of the streambed. If this is the case, cut the underlayment to fit the space and abut it to the nearby underlayment. Then cut a piece of flexible liner to fit the space; be sure to allot excess liner for pleating and tucking.

5 Overlap the catch basin liner with the stream liner, joining the two pieces with pond liner adhesive. For a good seal be sure the liners are dry before gluing them together, use plenty of adhesive, and overlap the liners by at least 2 inches. Allow the adhesive to dry according to package directions.

6 After the adhesive dries, pleat and tuck the flexible liner to take out the excess and help the liner lie smoothly along the course of the streambed and around the catch basin. The time spent folding the pond liner should be minimal, since it is not very noticeable once the project is completed. Use boulders to secure the folds in place.

7 With the liner in place, begin arranging the stones. The stones not only hide the liner, they also give the pond a finished look.

Using a cart, dolly, or the help of strong friends, move the largest stones into place. Bury them at the edge of the pond, covering them up so that only about half their height shows. Also position some of the stones in the stream where water will partially cover them. Next, begin edging the stream by placing medium and small stones in between the large

< **76** >

stones. This will give the stream an irregular, natural look. Finally, place small stones in the pond, covering the liner as much as possible.

8 Place the pump in the pump well or in the catch basin at the lowest part of the stream. (When buying the pump, work with your supplier to select one that is powerful enough to move water the length of the stream and the height of the slope.) Set the pump on a stone or brick so it will not take in silt from the bottom of the pond.

Next, run flexible tubing alongside the stream from the pump to the top of the watercourse. At the top of the watercourse, secure the tubing in place with stones, taking care to not smash or damage the tubing. Mask the tubing along the stream by weaving it among pond side marginals, or bury it in a trench.

9 Fill the catch basin with water. Plug the pump into a GFCI outlet and turn it on. Add more water and adjust the placement of the stones as needed to create the desired water flow and sound. You may also need to adjust the flow rate from the pump.

When you are satisfied with the stream's operation, disguise the tubing where it exits the water by placing stones over it. Be careful not to damage the tubing. Finally, landscape around the stream and catch basin with low-growing shrubs, perennials and small trees.

Notes

_____
_____
_____
_____
_____
_____

< 77 >

Container Garden

PROJECT BASICS

TIME: 2 hours

SKILL: easy

MATERIALS:
- a watertight container
- floating plants
- miniature water lily or other plants
- garden soil or aquatic planting mix
- pump
- fountain head

Potted water gardens are a step up from the tabletop gardens on page 64. Their larger size lets you grow a wider variety of plants or add a fountain to the garden. Use container water garden to accent a perennial border, make a focal point in a planting of herbs, or brighten a lightly shaded location.

Creating a potted water garden is easy. Any container will do, as long as it is watertight. If you would like to include fish in your garden, make sure you choose a container that is at least 12 inches deep.

< 78 >

❶ After putting the container in place, install the pump and fountain head. Pumps and fountains are not necessary for container gardens like those shown here, but they will promote clean water and healthy plants.

Attach the fountain head to the pump and place the pump in the bottom of the pot, setting it on bricks to hold the pump at the right level, if necessary. Drape the electrical cord over the back of the pot where it will not be visible.

❷ Add marginal plants to the water garden. Use bricks or flat stones as risers to elevate marginal and potted water plants. Taro, shown here, grows best when it is 6 inches or less below the water surface. Refrain from adding water lilies to a water feature with moving water; they grow best in still water. Fill the container with water. Plug the pump into a GFCI outlet and test water flow to ensure the fountain doesn't splash too much. Adjust the flow as necessary.

❸ Next, add floating plants to the garden. Use only a small number of floating plants; they will grow quickly and cover the surface of the garden. Thin floating plants as necessary to maintain a healthy ecosystem.

❹ Switch on the pump and readjust the fountain head if necessary to achieve the desired effect. Top off the water garden as needed. In winter, disassemble the container water garden. Store it in a covered area, or bring it inside and enjoy the sound of running water through winter.

< 79 >

Pond with Flexible Liner

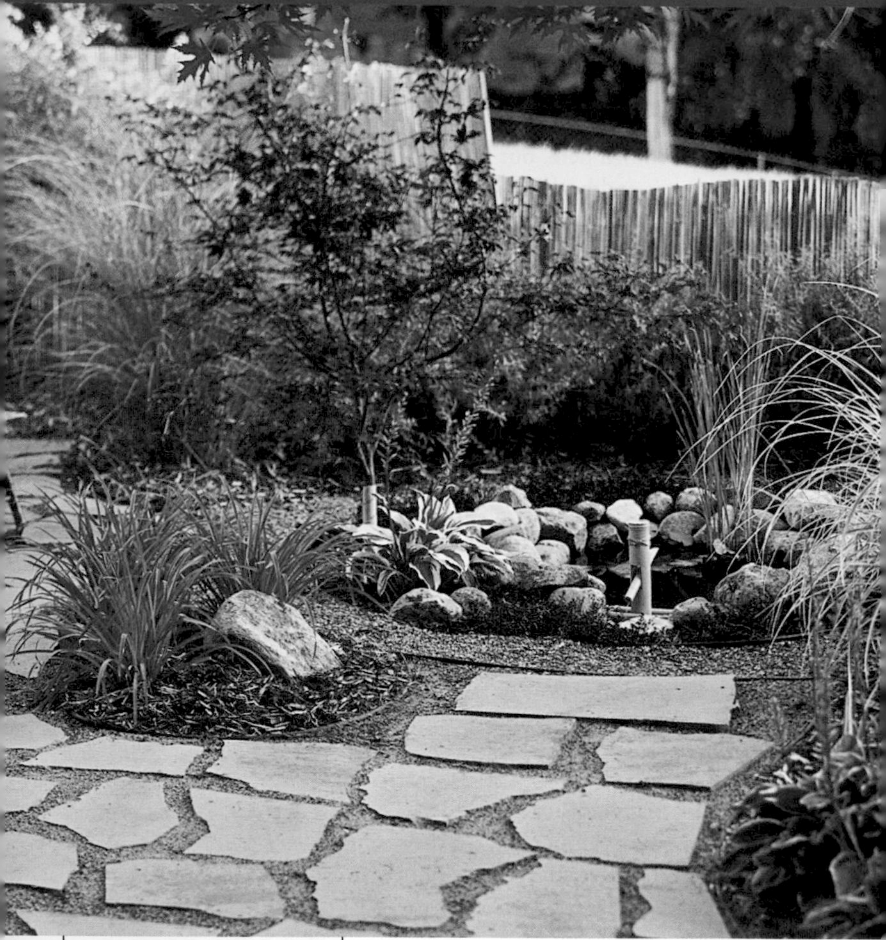

PROJECT BASICS
TIME: 2 days
SKILL: moderate

MATERIALS:
- underlayment
- liner
- stones of various sizes and pea gravel
- pump
- black plastic edging
- plants

Tucked beside a patio in a petite backyard, this small pond is a haven for wildlife, plants, and people. A gentle stream of water falls into the pond every few minutes from the bamboo fountain.

The pond is large enough to support fish. Goldfish, shubunkins, and koi are all good candidates. Add a deicer to the pond in winter.

1 Outline the shape of the pond and the circular path around the outside. Dig a hole for the pond with a shovel. (If your pond will be more than 2 feet deep, you may need to fence your yard; check local zoning regulations.) Dig a shelf about 4 inches deep and 6 inches wide around the perimeter of the pond.

2 Lay the underlayment in the excavated pond. Pleat it as necessary so that it covers the base and sides of the pond as well as the shelf.

With the underlayment in place, lay the flexible liner. Liner is easier to work with if you allow it to warm and soften in the sun for about an hour before you lay it. Pleat and tuck the liner around the edges of the pond. Hold it in place with large stones.

continued on page 82>>

Pond with Flexible Liner

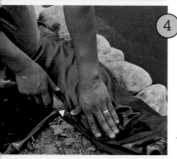

3 <<continued from page 81

3 Partially fill the pond, smoothing out wrinkles as the water flows. Tuck and pleat excess portions of the liner, repositioning rocks as needed.

4 Place rocks along the edge of the pond to permanently hold the liner in place and to camouflage it once the pond is filled. Here, medium-size rounded river stones were used. Cut off excess liner with a heavy-duty utility knife, leaving about 1 foot of liner extending beyond the rocks.

5 Wedge sections of permeable fabric, such as old towels or scraps of underlayment, behind the rocks to act as a filter to keep soil and debris from washing into the pond. Add more large rocks as necessary to secure the liner edge.

6 Cover the fabric with pea gravel, then place large rocks on top of the gravel. Finish filling the pond. Add water until it is 1 inch above the bottom of the large rocks ringing the pond.

7 Install the pump. Run the electrical cord out of the pond between the rocks. If necessary, connect it to a heavy-duty extension cord. For safety, thread the extension cord through a PVC pipe. Bury the pipe in a 6-inch-deep trench. Connect the cord to a GFCI outlet.

A deer scare, or shishi-odoshi, is a Japanese ornament designed to keep animals away from rice paddies and other cultivated areas. Also called a water hammer, a deer scare's simple form and operation make it a popular water garden feature as well. It may not ward off deer in your yard, but the sound of trickling water is soothing.

❶ Using a hacksaw or bandsaw, cut 2½-inch diameter bamboo to a 40-inch length. At the base of the bamboo, 15 inches from the end, drill a hole slightly larger in diameter than the tubing you will use to circulate the water. Push a rebar rod through the bamboo to hollow it out. This will be the upright pipe of the fountain.

Two inches from the top of the pipe, drill a hole that is slightly more than 1 inch in diameter through the front for the spout. About 6 inches below this hole, cut out a rectangular opening on both the front and back of the pipe for the movable hammer. Drill a ½-inch hole on each side of the rectangular hole where you can insert a bamboo pin on which the hammer will pivot.

For the spout, cut a 1-inch-diameter cane to 8 inches long. Prepare the hammer by cutting a 1½-inch-diameter pipe to a 20-inch-length. On each, cut the tips at an angle and hollow out the bamboo, leaving the flat end closed. About 12 inches from the angle cut on the hammer, drill a ½-diameter hole through the bamboo for the bamboo pin.

continued on page 84>>

< 83 >

Deer Scare

2 <<continued from page 83

❷ Thread the tubing through the hole in the upright pipe, then all the way up the pipe, out the spout hole, and into the spout. Insert the spout into the upright pipe. It should fit snugly. To secure the spout and add a Japanese-style decoration to the fountain, tightly wrap twine around the spout and the upright pipe.

❸ Next insert the hammer into the rectangular opening on the upright pipe. Insert the bamboo pin through the upright, through the hammer and out the other side of the upright. The hammer should move freely on the pin like a teeter totter. Cut the pin flush with the upright pipe or let it extend beyond the pipe on either side.

Finally attach the tubing to a pump. Using stones, bricks, or bamboo supports tied on either side of the upright pipe, position the deer scare in the pond. Check with a level to ensure it stands plumb. Switch on the pump. Adjust the pump flow so the water drips into the hammer. When the hammer is filled, it will tip down to spill the water into the pond.

< 85 >

① Water feature

IN EARLY SPRING clean out any debris that accumulated over winter. Skim leaves, fallen petals, and other floating plant matter from the bottom and surface of the pool with a net. Regularly skim off debris throughout spring and summer.

KEEP THE POND FILLED. Summer evaporation accounts for the loss of up to an inch of water per week. ❶ If your pond consistently loses more than this, look for and repair leaks. If you need to add water, fill the pond with just a trickle of water from a hose placed on the bottom of the pond. Don't add more than 10 percent of the total volume at any one time.

CONTROL ALGAE NATURALLY. ❷ Barley straw, which comes as pellets or in bales, releases a chemical that prevents or slows algae growth. Submerged plants and floating plants limit algae growth in two ways. For example, water hyacinth and water lettuce so effectively absorb nutrients from the water that they starve algae to death. ❸ Anarcharis and other submerged plants outcompete algae for oxygen.

Plants

IN SPRING return hardy aquatic plants to the pond if you removed them for the winter. Or if they overwintered in the deepest part of the pond, relocate them for the growing season.

SPRING IS THE BEST TIME to plant new marginal, submerged, and floating plants. It's also time to divide root-bound plants and repot the divisions.

< 86 >

AS THE GROWING SEASON PROGRESSES, remove spent flowers, yellowing foliage, and excess plant growth.

IN SUMMER feed water lilies, lotuses, and other nonsubmerged water garden plants with aquatic plant food.

RAKE OFF overexuberant floating plants, especially if they cover more than 60 percent of the water's surface. ❹ If algae gets out-of-hand, a toilet brush makes a nice skimmer for removing it.

AVOID USING INSECTICIDES. Pick off pests or blast them off plants with water from the garden hose. Remove and dispose of thoroughly infested or diseased plants.

❺ **CONTROL MOSQUITOES** by tossing Bt *(Bacillus thuringiensis)* granules or dunks (or tablets) into the water.

Equipment

IN SPRING reconnect the pump and filter if you stored it over winter.

CLEAN THE PUMP INTAKE WEEKLY; clean the filter, skimmer, and other accessories as needed for efficient operation.

Fish

IN SPRING as water begins to warm and fish resume activity, begin feeding them minimally with spring/fall high-carbohydrate food.

ADD NITRIFYING BACTERIA to guard against toxic buildup of ammonia from fish waste.

< **87** >

(1) Water feature

❶ DRAIN wall or freestanding fountains, using a pump to siphon the water. If possible, remove stone or ceramic components that might be damaged during the winter freeze/thaw cycle.

PROTECT a raised pond from ice damage by draining it to ground level.

Plants

BEFORE THE FIRST FROST, remove tropical lilies and other nonhardy plants from the pond and save them in a greenhouse pool or an indoor aquarium. You can also store tropical lilies in a cool, dark place in moist sand. Move tropical marginal plants indoors and enjoy them as houseplants in winter.

❷ DISCARD floating and tropical plants that you are not overwintering once frost makes them unsightly.

ONCE HARDY WATER PLANTS have been knocked out by frost, remove and dispose of their foliage. Cut upright plant stalks 1 to 2 inches above the water surface (wait until spring to cut cattails and grasses). Cut submerged plants to within 6 inches of their containers. Transfer hardy water plants to the deep zone of the pond for overwintering.

TRANSFER hardy water lilies to deeper water, where they won't freeze. Or remove foliage, wrap plants in moist newspaper and then loosely in plastic bags, and store them indoors in a dark, cool area.

< 88 >

Equipment

③ BEFORE LEAVES FALL install netting over the pond to prevent them from landing in the water and decaying there. Support the netting with 2×4s or beach balls. If you don't install netting, use a hand skimmer daily to remove leaves.

WHEN THE WATER TEMPERATURE DROPS below 50°F, remove, clean, and store your mechanical filter and pump.

IF THERE IS DANGER of the pond freezing solid, install a pond deicer to maintain an open spot in the water surface so that oxygen can enter the water. Oxygen in the water is necessary for overwintering plants and fish.

AVOID OPERATING THE PUMP during freezing weather, which can damage the pump, the pipes, and the fish. Allow the pump to continue working only if you live in a mild climate where ice is a temporary occurrence.

IN FALL, drain pipes to prevent them from freezing and cracking. Turn off the water supply.

Fish

DISCONTINUE FEEDING fish when the water temperature drops below 45°F. Resist the temptation to feed them during any midwinter warm spells. Cold temperatures quickly return, making the fish too cold to digest food. The undigested food spoils in the fish's guts, a sometimes fatal situation. Bring koi and other nonhardy fish indoors for the winter.

③

① Liner shows

PROBLEM: ❶ The pond is finished, but the liner sticks out below the edges.

SOLUTION: This often happens when the pond is not level and one side is higher than another. First, make sure the pond is full. If that doesn't solve the problem, check the level all around the pond with a carpenter's level and a 2×4 stretched across the pond. Disassemble the edging. Dig soil out from underneath the edge of the liner until all sides are level with each other. Relay the edging.

If this is too much work, consider planting evergreens or other sprawling plants along the rim of the pond to help conceal the liner.

Chlorine in water

PROBLEM: City tap water has chlorine and various minerals in it. Can it be used in a water garden or is a special source required?

SOLUTION: Chlorine dissipates from tap water in just a few days, or you can add a dechlorinator. After filling your water garden, let it sit for five to seven days before adding plants and fish. The minerals in the water will not harm aquatic life.

More of a concern to water gardeners are chloramines, powerful antibacterial agents that are added to (or occur naturally in) many local water supplies. Call your water supplier to ask if chloramines are present. If they are, treat water with chloramine remover before adding fish. The treatment also removes chlorine.

Muddy water

PROBLEM: ❷ Muddy water remains for several hours or even all day after a heavy rain.

SOLUTION: Muddy water, in itself, is usually not a problem, especially if the silt settles within a few hours. If it doesn't, however, the problem could be caused by soil erosion or

< 90 >

mud splashed into the pond by heavy rain. Check around the water feature, especially at its edging. Protect eroding soil by spreading gravel or organic mulch over it, or plant a ground cover in the problem area.

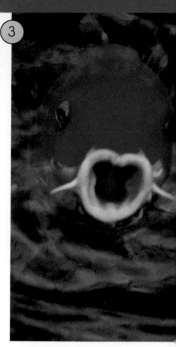

Smelly water

PROBLEM: The water has a foul smell.

SOLUTION: Bad smells from your pond mean that anaerobic bacteria have gotten out of hand. Poor aeration, a dead animal in the water, or an excess of uneaten fish food could be the cause.

Add a waterfall, fountain, or pump to the pond to increase aeration. Promptly remove dead or decaying plant matter and fish. Reduce the amount of food you give fish and don't feed them at all during hot weather. Keep the water feature topped off in warm weather so the water doesn't get murky. Reevaluate your ecosystem— adding filtering plants may help. In severe cases, a biological water filter may be the solution.

The pond is full of muck

PROBLEM: In autumn, fallen leaves and other plant debris fill the pond.

SOLUTION: Skim away fallen leaves daily so they don't have a chance to decay and pollute the water. If your pool or pond is located under a tree, consider stretching netting over the pond to catch the leaves. Be sure to remove these netted leaves regularly so they don't shade the water. If the leaves sink to the bottom of the pond, remove them with your hand or a lightweight plastic rake. Regular care is key to keeping the pond free of muck and debris.

Sick fish

PROBLEM: My fish are dying.

SOLUTION: If you see fish "gulping" at the water surface before they die, they are suffering from lack of oxygen. Install a pump with an aerator or air stone. Disease may also be the culprit. Move fish to a bucket of pond water and look for signs of disease: sluggishness, clamped fins, abnormal blotching or markings on their bodies, and ragged tails and fins. Take the fish to a professional for further diagnosis and treatment.

< 91 >

INDEX

< 92 >

< 93 >

< **94** >

This map of climate zones helps you select plants for your garden that will survive a typical winter in your region. The United States Department of Agriculture (USDA) developed the map, basing the zones on the lowest recorded temperatures across North America. Zone 1 is the coldest area and Zone 11 is the warmest.

Plants are classified by the coldest temperature and zone they can endure. For example, plants hardy to Zone 6 survive where winter temperatures drop to –10° F. Those hardy to Zone 8 die long before it's that cold. These plants may grow in colder regions but must be replaced each year. Plants rated for a range of hardiness zones can usually survive winter in the coldest region as well as tolerate the summer heat of the warmest one.

To find your hardiness zone, note the approximate location of your community on the map, then match the color band marking that area to the key.

HAWAII

AUSTRALIA

UNITED KINGDOM

Range of Average Annual Minimum Temperatures for Each Zone

Zone 1: Below -50° F (below -45.6° C)
Zone 2: -50 to -40° F (-45.5 to -40° C)
Zone 3: -40 to -30° F (-39.9 to -34.5° C)
Zone 4: -30 to -20° F (-34.4 to -28.9° C)
Zone 5: -20 to -10° F (-28.8 to -23.4° C)
Zone 6: -10 to 0° F (-23.3 to -17.8° C)
Zone 7: 0 to 10° F (-17.7 to -12.3° C)
Zone 8: 10 to 20° F (-12.2 to -6.7° C)
Zone 9: 20 to 30° F (-6.6 to -1.2° C)
Zone 10: 30 to 40° F (-1.1 to 4.4° C)
Zone 11: Above 40° F (above 4.5° C)